WONDERS of the SEA

WONDERS
of the
SEA

Kendall Haven

Merging Ocean Myth and Ocean Science

Illustrated by Julie Stringer

Wonders of Nature: Natural Phenomena in Science and Myth

A Member of the Greenwood Publishing Group

Westport, Connecticut • London

Library of Congress Cataloging-in-Publication Data

Haven, Kendall F.
    Wonders of the sea / by Kendall Haven.
      p.   cm.—(Wonders of nature)
    Includes bibliographical references and index.
    ISBN 1–59158–279–2 (pbk.)
    1. Ocean—Study and teaching (Elementary) 2. Ocean—Study and teaching
(Middle school) 3. Ocean—Mythology—Study and teaching (Elementary) 4.
Ocean—Mythology—Study and teaching (Middle school) I. Title.
II. Wonders of nature (Libraries Unlimited)
    GC31.H38   2005
    551.46—dc22   2005044250

British Library Cataloguing in Publication Data is available.

Library of Congress Catalog Card Number: 2005044250
ISBN: 1–59158–279–2

First published in 2005

Libraries Unlimited, 88 Post Road West, Westport, CT 06881
A Member of the Greenwood Publishing Group, Inc.
www.lu.com

Printed in the United States of America

The paper used in this book complies with the
Permanent Paper Standard issued by the National
Information Standards Organization (Z39.48–1984).

10 9 8 7 6 5 4 3 2 1

Special Thanks

I owe a special thank you to a number of people and groups who helped me either with the stories or the science information for this book. In particular, a huge thank you to Dan Keding, a good friend and owner of the most extensive and comprehensive private collection of myths and fables in the country, and to Jeff Gere, who helped connect me with a host of gracious people during my efforts to collect Pacific rim myths.

I also owe a big thank you to the librarians and the Sonoma State University library and to a number of people at the Oregon State School of Oceanography for their help in gathering and verifying the science information in this book.

A personal thank you goes to Sharon Coatney for initially connecting this book with me and for her visionary work in shaping and steering this series to completion. Finally, I owe countless thanks to my proofreaders: Roni Berg, the love of my life, and Nanette von Berg.

Dedication

I dedicate this book to all who ever gazed upon the ocean, had their hearts lifted by its pounding rhythms, and wondered about the rolling seas with a deep longing and a nagging curiosity.

Contents

CONTENTS

Illustrations

Introduction

I made a guest appearance in a sixth-grade classroom recently. Because of my background in oceanography, I was asked to talk about the science of ocean currents. The kids in this class sat resigned, unenthused, slumped back in their chairs. It had the potential to be a very long hour. So I started by saying, "I want to tell you a story."

The change in the room was physical, palpable. The room was suddenly charged with electric energy. All of the students sat up higher and leaned forward.

Stories engage, enthuse, excite. Stories are a delight, a gift, a treat. Why not use the power of myth and story to engage students in serious science discussion and research?

Do myth and science belong together? Absolutely. What we now call myth represented, at one time, the best explanation available for the nature of the world that surrounds us. Much of what we now call science may, in some future eon, be regarded as myth and fantasy by those whose understanding goes far beyond our own. Gazing from ancient myth to modern science allows us to chart our human progress. It shows us where we have come from and who we were. It gives us a perspective from which to appreciate the benefits and majesty of the sciences that have led us to where we are.

Both myths and science attempt to answer the grand mysteries of nature—where things and beings came from, how they got here, why they act as they do, and the purpose of life. Myths explain things through story. Science explains them through empirical observation, controlled experiments, and precise calculation.

Science provides factual information and understanding. Stories create context and relevance for that information within the human mind. Stories inspire and captivate and open the door to follow-up science activity.

By definition, a myth is a traditional story or legend, especially one concerning fabulous or supernatural beings, giving expression to early beliefs and perceptions and often explaining natural phenomena or the origins of some aspect of a people or nature. Myths were (and still are) created as entertainment with a serious purpose. They were supposed to explain some origin or instruct community members in essential beliefs, attitudes, behavior, history, and values.

The blending of myth and science is nowhere more appropriate than in the churning oceans. The rolling, pounding seas are, and have always been, a vast mystery to us poor land creatures. Oceans seem to extend forever across the sweeping horizons and dwarf humans and even the land itself. Oceans cover over 70% of the Earth's surface. Ocean waters change from placid and playful aquamarine transparency that beckons snorkelers and swimmers into raging gray-green monster swells that threaten even the mightiest ships on the seas and pound mercilessly and terrifyingly against the shore.

Underneath that mirror-like ocean surface lie unknown, unseen, and almost unimaginable worlds. Lobsters walk, fish swim, sharks prowl, turtles dive, whales romp, and eels slither. Octopuses may reach arm spans of 200 feet down there where we can't see. Giant squid grow longer than five school busses. Whole species live, grow, and die without ever being seen or detected by humans.

Underneath the ocean's surface, life explodes in grand profusion. But we land folk can't see it and can't easily reach it, and we can barely begin to imagine it. We drop lines and nets into the unseen depths. Sometimes we haul them back up loaded with fish. Sometimes not. We seem to have little control over the outcome. So the oceans remain a gnawing mystery.

Ocean waters, molecule by molecule, are indestructible and survive forever—a feat incomprehensible to those of us who live out our lives in less than the blink of a geologic eye. Any molecule of ocean water could wind up lapping against the shore of a hundred different countries or it could evaporate and rain down on any spot on Earth. It might have done so a million times.

The water dinosaurs drank is still here. Rain that fell on the first humanoids 3 million years ago is still here. So is the ocean water that washed over the first living plant almost 4 billion years ago. That same water might fall on you in the next rain shower or gurgle out of your faucet when you turn the spigot. Next time you pour a glass of water, pause to wonder where that water has been, how many times it has cycled through the oceans, and what amazing things it has seen. It is the stuff of mysteries and the natural fodder for myths.

The oceans touch and effect us all, and that makes them even more mysterious. Water makes up more than two-thirds of your body weight. Your blood and tears are salty—just like the ocean. We can not drink salty ocean water. We need to drink fresh water. But inside, we are made up of salt water—just like the ocean. We may feel separated from the oceans. We may feel that the ocean is a dangerous and alien place. But inside we seem to be tightly linked to our saltwater origins. And that makes the oceans even more alluring and mysterious for us curious humans.

I wrote this book to introduce and explain some of the major concepts of modern ocean science by gazing at them through the wonders and intrigue of ocean myths. This book forms a bridge between the exciting world of mythic story and science's logic and precision.

To do that, I have picked eleven aspects of the ocean that lend themselves to myth and are also important to a science curriculum study of the oceans. For each, I compare the beliefs inherent in the myths with our current scientific understanding of the ocean. No story presented here comes from a single source. I have tracked multiple sources for all, and I have tried to fashion the common elements of those various sources into a unified version to present here.

Enjoy these mythic stories. Marvel at the science and reality of the oceans. Revel in the glorious mysteries that still lurk in the uncharted ocean depths. Then seek out your own mysteries and myths to explore, share, and revel in.

1 ························ Origin of the Seas

——————— MYTHS ABOUT THE SEA'S ORIGINS

The sea is full of mysteries. What lives under the surface? How wide is the sea? What lies on the other side? Where do ocean waves and tides come from? What makes the seas act as they do? But first among these mysteries has always been the very existence of the seas. Where did the oceans come from? How long have the seas been here?

Myths to explain the origins of the seas were, of course, closely tied to myths explaining the origins of the land and of the planet itself. These creation myths can be split into two types.

In the more common of these types, the sea exists first and the myth explains how the land was created from the sea. In these myths, inhabitants—usually living somehow in the sky—are distressed by a lack of a suitable living place. Someone—usually someone of no seeming importance or significance—dives to the mud at the bottom of the sea and drags up the first land (and thereby becomes a hero).

The first line of the creation myth of the Hat Creek Indians of the Pacific Northwest reads, "In the beginning there was nothing but water." A Cherokee myth first mentions *Galun'lati*, the Sky Vault, and then says, "A great distance below, more than seven handbreadths beneath *Galun'lati*, was a world of water." Earth is later created from the soft mud at the bottom of this ocean.

A myth from the Pomo of Northern California begins, "At first it was dark. There was neither wind nor rain. There were no people or animals. In the middle of the endless water . . ." And in a myth of the Onondaga of Northeast America, "Before the Earth existed, there was only water." In each of these stories, one lone diver—in the Onondaga myth a tiny muskrat—dives to the bottom of the sea and brings up mud to create land. A Hawaiian creation myth begins, "Kane, God of Creation, picked up a vast calabash floating in the wide sea. . . ." The sea exists and Kane creates sky and land from it. In the Bible, God created the seas before the heavens and Earth.

But these creation myths do not explain how the seas came to be. They begin with the sea already in existence. The second type of creation myth begins with land already existing and explains how the oceans came to be.

These myths typically rely on the mischief, greed, or misdeeds of a character to trigger catastrophic events that create the sea in a great flood. In one especially inventive story from Thailand, villagers decide to build bigger and bigger kites to win a kite-flying tournament. A clever man, helped by a gang of children, builds a kite bigger than houses, bigger than fields, bigger than valleys. A great storm blows in and lifts this enormous kite. The man and the children try to hold on, clutching at trees, grass, rocks, and the ground itself. But the storm lifts the kite high into the sky, pulling people and a great chunk of the Earth with it. The hole left behind forms the Bay of Siam. The bay fills with water that bubbles up from below and the water spills over to create the oceans. The chunk of Earth flies up to become the Moon. The kite sails even higher to become a constellation of stars in the twinkling night sky.

In a Venezuelan myth, the sea is trapped in a greedy pelican's egg. The pelican wants to hoard all the fish for himself. A curious and mischievous boy cracks open the egg and out spills the ocean to cover everything except the mountaintops that become islands. In a Yurok myth, Thunder and Earthquake are worried that without water the people will not have enough to eat and will not be able to live. Earthquake stomps off to find water. He sinks the land as he goes and that allows the ocean to flood in.

The myth presented below comes from the Tiano people of the Greater Antilles, Jamaica, and Haiti in the Caribbean Islands. Fryer Ramon Pane first wrote this story down in Hispanola, in the Dominican Republic, more than 500 years ago. Christopher Columbus commissioned Pane to record the beliefs, traditions, and customs of the Tiano people, one of the first cultures he encountered in "the New World." The myth uses bravery, magical intervention, anger of vengeful Gods, parents' undying love, and greedy children to create the oceans and establish the seas as the principal source of sustenance and food. Life comes from the sea.

"How the Sea Began," a Myth from the Dominican Republic

In the beginning of time, before the land was surrounded by sea, in a place called Zuania (South America), there stood four great mountains. One of these mountains was called Boriquen, Land of Brave Men. In the village of Coabey on the side of that mountain lived an old man, Yaya, with his wife, Itiba, and their only son, Yayael. Yayael was a skilled hunter.

Yayael hunted with a bow his father had carved from tabonuco wood. It is said that the tabonuco tree is the home of spirits and that its wood holds magic power.

This may be true, because when Yayael hunted he always brought back game. The people of Coabey ate well, even when hunters from other villages came back empty-handed.

While hunting one day, Yayael noticed that the sky darkened in the east. Then a flock of swallows flew before the lowering clouds and circled low around his head, flapping and beating their wings. Yayael knew this was a warning that Guabancex, the terrible goddess of hurricanes, had awoken and was angry at Yayael's magical hunting success. She was coming to take revenge.

Yayael quickly hid his bow and remaining arrows under a large rock and ran toward the village, hoping to reach safety before the screeching winds and pelting rain overtook him.

Guabancex struck with tremendous force. Winds raged for hours. Trees that had stood for all of time were uprooted and tossed aside like kindling. Every house in the village was ripped apart and flattened.

The villagers had been working in their fields when the hurricane struck and sought shelter in a cave. When the winds died to a moan and a whimper, the people ventured from the cave to find their village destroyed. Yaya and Itiba waited for Yayael to return, but Yayael did not appear.

Yaya went to search for his son. He found the bow and arrows where Yayael hid them, but no trace of Yayael could be found.

When Itiba saw her husband return with their son's hunting bow, she screamed out Yayael's name and fell down weeping at Yaya's feet. Yaya reverently placed Yayael's bow and arrows in a large gourd and sat down beside his wife and wept with her.

The villagers helped one another rebuild the village. When the time for grieving was over, they helped Yaya and Itiba hang the gourd from the ceiling of their hut. There the bow and arrows would be safe—just in case Yayael's spirit should wish to visit them.

Yaya and the other village men picked up their bows and trudged out to hunt, since they could no longer count on Yayael to bring home meat to feed the village.

Though the men hunted every day, they never brought home enough. All were hungry. Even the children, who were always fed first, became thin and sickly.

In desperation one evening, Yaya asked Itiba to lower the gourd that held Yayael's weapons. "I want to see our son's bow," he said. "Perhaps it still holds some power of the tabonuco."

As Itiba lowered the gourd to the floor, it tipped just a little. Out splashed many plump fish. Yaya and Itiba were astonished. They had never before seen such fish—large and silvery and still breathing, as if freshly pulled from a stream—but bigger, plumper, and unlike any fish that ever swam in the streams or rivers of their land. Itiba cooked the fish and invited the whole village to share the meal.

The villagers rejoiced in their good fortune and sang "Bahari Yayael!" ("We honor you, Yayael!") And they went to bed with full, happy stomachs for the first time in weeks.

The next day the villagers marched out to work in the fields. They left four boys to guard the gourd with Yayael's bow and arrows that Itiba had re-hung from the ceiling of his hut.

But the boys soon grew both curious and hungry. The higher the sun climbed, the hungrier and more curious they became. One boy stood on tiptoe and tried to peer into the gourd. Then a second tried to climb up to see inside. Together, the four boys climbed, and tugged, and pulled, and brought the gourd down to the floor.

Out flopped four beautiful fish—just the right size for four hungry boys.

The boys cooked and ate the fish. Then they ate four more. Then, singing praises to Yayael, they ate yet four more. Now happily stuffed, they fell asleep.

The boys awoke to the sounds of the villagers returning from the fields. Afraid of being caught, they hurried to re-hang the gourd from the ceiling. In their haste, they failed to secure the rope. The rope knot slipped. The gourd fell to the ground and broke open with a wrenching "Crack!"

Water rushed out of the broken gourd. Yaya and Itiba's hut was instantly flooded. A towering wave swept the boys to the edge of the village and left them choking and gasping at the feet of the villagers.

The water tasted of salt, the boys said, just like the salt of the tears shed for Yayael.

But water continued to pour and to gush from the broken gourd like a raging fountain. A torrent raced down the path toward the valley below. It washed out the villagers' fields and swept away trees and boulders.

Fish of all sizes, colors, shapes, and imagining swam out of the gourd and were carried by the current—large fish, small fish, eels, squids, sharks, jellyfish, and all manner of sea creatures swam out of the gourd to fill the salty water with life.

The villagers gathered high on the mountaintop and watched as the waters rose to cover Zuania. When at last the water stopped rising and their old village lay deep under the sea, they saw that the mountain was now an island, surrounded by the endless life of the sea.

The villagers dressed themselves festively and celebrated with music and dance. They knew they would never go hungry as long as there were fish in the sea. Yayael, the great hunter, had again provided for his village.

And that is how the sea began.

– THE SCIENCE OF THE ORIGIN OF THE SEAS

The following beliefs are either directly stated or strongly implied in the presented myth. Here is what modern science knows about the aspects of the seas explained by each belief.

BELIEF: The land existed before the oceans. (Or was it the oceans that were created first?)

So which came first? The chicken or the egg? The sea or the land?

Six billion years ago, give or take several hundred million, hot gasses and space dust condensed into a planet—the Earth—as they spun around a glowing, pulsing star—the Sun. Over the next billion years that hot, molten mass cooled so that its crust hardened and solidified into solid rock. But the planet was not quiet. Volcanoes ripped the crust apart. Molten lava and gasses boiled across the land. An atmosphere of gasses began to form above the planet. Water vapor (spewed into the sky from the volcanoes and vent gasses) filled that atmosphere and formed into thick clouds.

It began to rain. For centuries and eons as the volcanoes blasted steam and glowing lava into the air, the clouds poured down torrents of rain. The rain gathered into lakes and rivers that tumbled toward the lowest lands, filling those to become the oceans. Virtually all the water that will ever exist on Earth existed back billions of years ago when the oceans first formed. Water cycles through oceans, clouds, rivers, dinosaurs, trees, evaporation, polar ice caps, humans, and back to the oceans.

That is science's best estimate of how the land and oceans formed. What does it mean? First, land existed before the oceans were made. Second, it took millions (probably hundreds of millions) of years for the oceans to form. Third, water isn't created or destroyed. It cycles and re-cycles through the Earth. The water you drink today is really billions of years old. It might have been lapped up by a wooly mammoth, a diplodocus (a dinosaur), or a saber-toothed tiger. It might have been sucked out of the Earth by a prehistoric redwood tree. It might have been locked for a million years into the ice structure of an Alaskan gla-cier. Two hundred thousand years ago an early human might have looked at his reflection in a pool that held one of the water drops you drink today.

There is still some water below the crust of the Earth. It reaches the oceans and atmosphere when volcanoes erupt and when undersea vents pour forth their fiery steam and gas.

The Tiano myth was correct. Land existed before the oceans, though the story was wrong in its description of how the ocean was formed.

Ocean Terms

There are many terms we use to describe different parts and aspects of the ocean. You will find it helpful to know and use them. Scientists use these terms to divide huge oceans into smaller pieces that are easier to study and describe, and into parts that are similar to each other.

Scientists use three systems to describe the oceans. The first looks at the geography of the surface of the ocean. The second looks at a profile of the ocean floor. The final system looks at the ocean water itself and divides it into vertical zones depending on how much sunlight filters down into each zone.

First, scientists describe the oceans by their surface geography.

Ocean

An ocean is a large body of water. The word *ocean* comes from the Greek word *okeanos*, meaning "river." Early Greeks believed that the ocean (for example, the Mediterranean Sea) was a great river.

There have traditionally been four oceans on Earth: the Pacific, Atlantic, Indian, and Arctic Oceans. Some scientists say that the Antarctic Ocean should be called a separate ocean. New surface and satellite data have shown that the strong currents that circle the Antarctic continent do not readily mix with the waters of the South Pacific or South Atlantic Oceans. Since it acts like a separate body of water, they say that the Antarctic should be called a separate ocean. However, oceans are also supposed to be divided from each other by continents—the great landmasses of the world. No landmasses separate the Antarctic Ocean from the Pacific, Atlantic, or Indian Oceans, so the common thinking still is that it does not qualify as a separate ocean.

The oceans cover 71% of the Earth's surface and contain 97% of Earth's 350 million cubic miles of water. While oceans are separated by continents, they are still interconnected so that water flows freely from ocean to ocean. The four recognized oceans are:

> **Pacific Ocean.** The Pacific is by far the biggest and deepest of the oceans. Covering 64 million square miles with an average depth of

FIGURE 1.1 · The Four Oceans

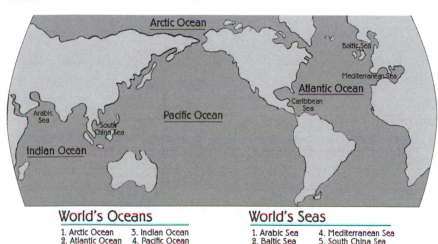

World's Oceans

1. Arctic Ocean	3. Indian Ocean
2. Atlantic Ocean	4. Pacific Ocean

World's Seas

1. Arabic Sea	4. Mediterranean Sea
2. Baltic Sea	5. South China Sea
3. Caribbean Sea	

13,737 feet, it stretches at its widest point from Panama to the Philippine Islands and from Alaska to Antarctica. The deepest trench in the world (the Marianas Trench) plunges six miles down along the western edge of the Pacific. That's six times deeper than the world-famous Grand Canyon! The Pacific Ocean also features far more active undersea volcanoes than any other ocean. The *el niño* and *la niña* temperature shifts that so radically change weather over much of the Earth happen in the central and southern parts of the eastern Pacific.

Atlantic Ocean. Less than half the size of the Pacific Ocean, the Atlantic Ocean is also 3,000 feet shallower. However, sandwiched between Europe and North America and between Africa and South America, the Atlantic is growing wider at the rate of about one inch each year while the Pacific is slowly shrinking. The Atlantic contains two great features. One is the mid-Atlantic Ridge, a mountainous ridge—like an S-shaped, raised, spiny backbone—that curves down the middle of the ocean from Iceland into the far reaches of the South Atlantic. This ridge is the boundary between Earth's giant crustal plates and is where new crust boils and erupts from the mantle below. The mid-Atlantic Ridge connects with an inverted Y-shaped ridge that stretches across the Indian Ocean, swings around Australia, and links into the Pacific rise. In all, this undersea mountain ridge stretches more than 40,000 miles, marks the boundary between eight major plates of the Earth's crust, and produces more than ten cubic miles of new crust each year.

The Atlantic's second feature is the Gulf Stream, a giant river within the ocean that pumps billions of gallons of warm tropical water north along east coast of the United States and across to Northern Europe before cooling and drifting south along the European coast.

Indian Ocean. Barely a third the size of the Pacific Ocean, the Indian Ocean covers only 24 million square miles. Because most of this ocean lies in the tropics, it is the warmest of the oceans, with summer surface temperatures reaching 80 degrees F over much of its area. Fewer scientific studies have been conducted in the Indian Ocean than in any other ocean. For example, only three small spots along the 6,000-mile-long mid-ocean ridge in the Indian Ocean have ever been surveyed.

Arctic Ocean. Shallow (average depth is only 3,250 feet) and cold (water temperatures average 29 degrees F), the Arctic Ocean circles the North Pole bordered by Alaska, Canada, Greenland, Russia, and Norway. Covering only 4.7 million square miles, the Arctic is tiny compared to other oceans. Though shallow, the Arctic is difficult to study because it is completely ice-covered each winter and partially ice-covered all year. The Arctic is the only ocean you can walk across!

It is also the noisiest ocean, with ice floes grinding, breaking, and crashing into each other.

Sea

Many people use ocean and sea interchangeably. But to scientists they are different. Seas are smaller, identifiable bodies of water, usually partially or wholly encircled by land. Examples include the Mediterranean Sea, Caspian Sea, Arabian Sea, Aegean Sea, Caribbean Sea, Coral Sea, South China Sea, Bering Sea, and North Sea. There are more than forty seas on Earth.

But a sea doesn't have to be surrounded by land as long as it forms a specific, identifiable body of water. The Sargasso Sea is an area in the middle of the tropical Atlantic Ocean hated by sailors for its lack of wind, its stagnant waters, and its burning sun. Many a sailor has died of dehydration and hunger while drifting week after week, becalmed, on the seaweed-coated Sargasso Sea. Currents and winds flow all around the Sargasso, but they do not mix with the trapped water of that sea.

Bay

A bay is a smaller coastal body of water enclosed by land on three sides, open to an ocean or sea on the fourth, and in which fresh water and seawater do not mix. Thus, bay water is approximately the same saltiness as ocean water. Often estuaries are mislabeled and called bays. San Francisco Bay, for example, is not a bay. It is an estuary because three rivers flow into the bay and mix their fresh water with salt water.

Estuary

An estuary is a coastal bay in which there is significant mixing of fresh and salt water so that the salinity of the estuary slowly increases from near zero parts-per-thousand (ppt) on the inland end toward ocean salinity levels near its mouth. The lower Hudson River is an estuary. So is San Francisco Bay and the Chesapeake Bay. Rivers flow into estuaries. Estuaries empty into the sea.

Estuaries are of particular interest and importance because they account for so much of the oceans biological productivity, especially the production of plankton (microscopic floating ocean plants). The marine species that bloom in estuaries exist no where else on Earth. The oceans

FIGURE 1.2 • Profile of the Ocean Bottom

depend on these species and on estuaries to be the biological engines that drive ocean primary productivity. However, estuaries are also where major cities hug the coast. Estuaries are where people want to fill in the mud flats and acres of sea grasses to build more houses, shipping docks, and businesses. Estuaries are where people dump the most pollutants. Estuaries are where humans and nature come into the most dangerous and direct conflict. Estuaries are one of our most precious—and most fragile—resources, and the resource that is stressed and destroyed by human action more than any other.

Scientists also describe the ocean by dividing the ocean floor into five zones.

Coast

The coast includes the land along the shore, the shoreline from high tide to low tide, and the shallow waters that hug the coast, coastal bays, and estuaries. The coast is where we humans live, vacation, and play. The coast is where we place piers, jetties, ports, wharves, factories, canneries, hotels, and amusement parks. The coast is the boundary between the land world and the ocean world.

Continental Shelf

Along the shore of every continent lies a shelf of shallow water. Water depths along this shelf rarely exceed 600 feet. During past major ice ages (when the sea level was much lower than it is today), these shelves were exposed to the air and formed the coasts of the continents. Continental shelves are etched with hills, plains, and river valleys and all the features you would find on land. Continental shelves are really submerged parts of the continent.

Continental shelves are the most productive areas of the oceans, housing most of the important fishing grounds. The shelves, because they are next to the coastal lands, are also where humans dump their waste, their urban runoff and treatment sludge, and their garbage. Every year, the tons of waste we humans dump into the oceans is greater than the total tons of fish our fishermen pull out of the oceans.

Continental Slope

The continental shelf ends where steep slopes (and often sheer cliffs) plunge into the blackness of the deep oceans. Often several miles high, this slope separates the continents from the deep ocean floor. How impressive this slope must look to the fish swimming by! Shaped much like the sides of mesas in the Southwest, but often twenty times as high, the slopes surround the deep oceans like the walls of a giant swimming pool.

Continental Rise

The continental rise is a gentler sloping part of the ocean floor that connects the deep ocean floor to the continental slope. Like the foothills of a mountain range, the slope is a transition zone between the mostly flat ocean floor and the steep walls of the slope.

Deep Ocean Floor (the Abyssal Plain)

The deep ocean floor, called the *abyssal plain,* is mostly a flat plain— but one pockmarked with towering volcanic mountains, sea mounts rising like spires from the floor, rippling expanses of sand that stretch for thousands of miles, buckled ridges, deep trenches that plunge far deeper and more precipitously than any canyon on land, wide patches of mud, waving forests of deep ocean plants, and long mountain ranges. Vents hiss steam and hot gasses to boil the surrounding water.

The deep oceans are a mysterious and alien world whose ecosystem is

FIGURE 1.3 · Three Zones of the Ocean Water

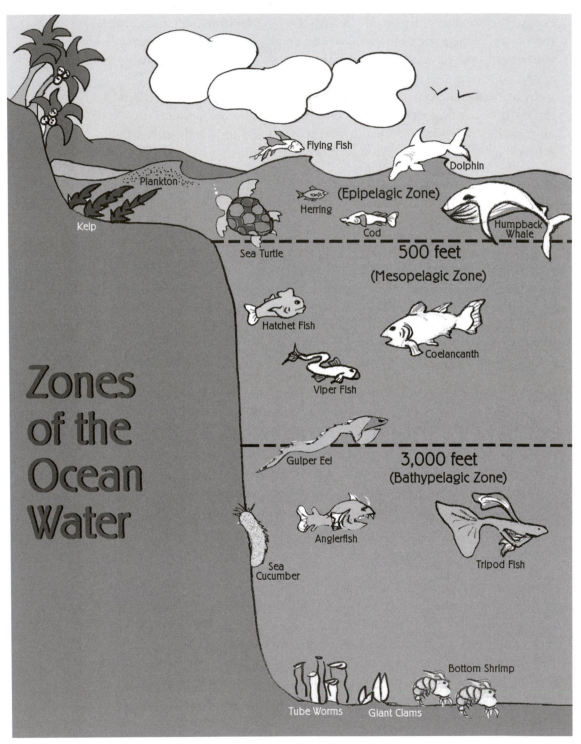

as different as can be imagined from those of the land environments in which we live.

Finally, scientists also divide the ocean waters themselves, vertically, into three different zones. This division scheme is useful because different types of plants and animals live in each of these layers of the ocean

Epipelagic (Top Layer)

The sunlit upper layers of the ocean cover the top 400 to 500 feet of the ocean. Sunlight permeates this layer. This is the realm of ocean plants—phyto- and zooplankton, seaweeds, kelps, and sea grasses. Plankton are the equivalent of grass, bushes, and trees on land. Ocean plants (algae) support the entire oceanic ecosystem. Because the ocean plants live in this top layer of the water, most of the fish live here also. The epipelagic layer includes the continental shelf plus the surface layers of the deep oceans.

Mesopelagic (Twilight Layer)

The mesopelagic zone is a dim, twilight world of shadows that extends from a depth of about 500 feet to around 3,000 feet. Not enough sunlight penetrates into this mid-ocean layer to allow plants (plankton) to grow. Many of the ocean's giant mystery fish, such as the giant squid, vicious looking dragonfish, and the fifty-foot-long oarfish, live in this zone of the ocean's water column.

Scientists have always thought the mesopelagic zone was a desert, nearly devoid of life. However, almost every submersible that has descended through these waters has reported meeting fish. It now appears that this dim world of vague shadows may be a far more lively place than once thought.

Bathypelagic (Deep Ocean)

The midnight black deep oceans are all waters below 3,000 feet. No sunlight reaches these waters. But (surprisingly) many fish and plants thrive in this perpetual darkness. Many of the deep ocean fish make their own lights, looking like the running lights on a truck. Ocean plants proliferate along the ocean floor—all without sunlight and without oxygen, the basis of plant life on land. Forests of tubeworms and fern-like plants thrive—especially near any ocean vents (rips and holes in the ocean floor where hot steam and gasses belch up from the molten magma chambers below). Few humans have seen this part of the ocean and less than one thousandth of 1% of the deep ocean floor has been explored. It is still a place of mystery and surprise for modern scientists. Science knows more about the surface of Mars, the Moon, Venus, and the large moons of Saturn than about the deep oceans of our own planet.

BELIEF: Oceans were created all at once.

Clearly this belief is not true. The oceans were created over millions—even hundreds of millions—of years. Water molecules trapped in the molten interior of Earth had to work their way to the surface, riding outward through volcanic tubes and steam vents. The process was slow. But then, it takes many volcanic eruptions and many hissing, bubbling oceanic vents to deliver 350 million cubic miles of water to the surface of the Earth!

BELIEF: Oceans are essential to the emergence and existence of life on land.

The myth said that the people cheered and celebrated when the oceans were created, even though those oceans destroyed their village and fields as well as the deep valleys and rolling plains on which they had always hunted and gathered food. This implies that the Tiano people believed (as did many other native peoples) that life and sustenance sprang from, and depended on, the oceans.

Scientists are now convinced that life on this planet did start in the oceans. Here is science's best estimate of the progression of life:

4 billion years ago	Bacteria developed in the oceans.
3 billion years ago	The first plants (ocean algae) developed.
600 million years ago	Oceanic animals began to develop.
470 million years ago	The first plants edged out of the sea to live on land.

First simple bacteria and then one-cell planktonic plants and tiny creatures formed. Then came a profusion of plants—algae and kelps. Over time larger fish developed. Then plants moved on shore. Then came reptiles that first crawled out of the seas onto dry land. Life started in the seas and spread to land. Now many of the land animals (and humans) depend on and eat the fish, mammals, and kelp that live in the sea.

Moreover, life on land depends on oxygen and water. Both come primarily from the ocean. Since 97% of all water is in the oceans, almost all evaporation comes from ocean water. Evaporated water forms clouds that create rain. That rain is the source of all surface fresh water.

Plants "exhale" oxygen as part of their photosynthesis process. Most of the Earth's plant life exists in the surface layers of the oceans. Thus, most of the Earth's supply of oxygen comes from the oceans. Life on land does depend on life in the oceans.

Finally, ocean currents control the flow and distribution of heat around the planet, which affects weather and climate. When the Sun's heat strikes Earth, it is stored primarily in the tropical oceans. Ocean currents move that heat around the globe. The Gulf Stream brings heat to northern Europe and keeps its climate much warmer than most other areas at the same latitude. The west coast of the United States is cooled by cold water currents from Alaska that bring bitter-cold winter rain and summer fog to San Francisco, California. The oceans control weather and climate on land.

The myth and belief are correct. Life on Earth depends on the oceans.

· ·

BELIEF: The oceans are now as they have always been.

The entire surface of Earth is constantly in motion. Slow motion, but motion nonetheless. The oceans (like the continents) are forever changing shape. The Atlantic Ocean is growing wider by an inch a year. (The Atlantic is now twenty-two yards wider than when Columbus first crossed it.) The Pacific Ocean is slowly shrinking. The skinny Red Sea is expanding and in 200 million years will be as wide as the Atlantic is now.

What moves the continents around and changes the shape of oceans? Plate tectonics. The Earth's outer crust is broken into about twenty separate chunks called plates. Plates glide over the molten mantel below, pulling away from each other and crashing into each other like cars on a bumper car ride. Mountainous mid-oceanic ridges form where two plates are pulling apart (for example, the mid-Atlantic ridge). New crust flows up from the mantle along these ridges to fill in the gap left as plates move apart. Tectonic plates crash together in other places along the edges of oceans. One plate rides up on top of the other, pushing the edge of the bottom plate back down into the mantle. Volcanoes and deep ocean trenches mark these areas that are called *convergence zones.*

As continents slowly move, oceans also change shape. But the ocean changes in other ways as well. Sea level rises and falls over eons of time. During past ice ages, sea level was as much as 800 feet lower than it now is. Back then, you could walk from Long Island straight north to Massachusetts. Much of what is now the Gulf of Mexico was dry land. San Francisco Bay did not exist. The continental shelves were part of the land of the continents.

Ocean currents also shift over time. The famous Gulf Stream current that flows north along the east coast of the United States and carries warm water to northern Europe once flowed from north to south and carried frigid arctic water south toward the equator as the Alaska current now does along the U.S. west coast.

El niños and *la niñas* (two periodic phenomena of the Pacific Ocean) change the surface temperatures and current patterns in the tropical Pacific Ocean and thereby change weather patterns all over the world.

No, oceans never stay the same. Oceans are churning, changing, flowing, dynamic, and exciting places!

BELIEF: The bottom of the sea is covered with mud and is a barren mud-scape.

Many of the origin myths say that land is created from mud pulled up from the bottom of the sea. Is mud what is down there? How did early people know?

For thousands of years humans sailed over on the seas and fished in the seas. But no human saw what the bottom of the oceans looked like. They only saw the bottom of shallow coastal waters. People imagined that the ocean bottom was covered with mud. But no one knew, even though many humans longed to probe below the surface and to explore the wondrous undersea world.

Submarines were invented during the American Revolutionary War. Those subs were powered by bicycle-style pedals and could only submerge a few feet beneath the surface. The first practical submarines were invented in the early twentieth century, but they could only descend a few hundred feet below the surface. Frenchman Jacques Cousteau invented scuba gear in 1945, but no one was able to descend more than 200 feet in scuba gear until well into the 1970s. The first submersible that allowed humans to reach the deep ocean floor and take a look around wasn't built until the late 1960s!

Just think—the ocean floor had been down there for billions of years; no human saw it until less than forty years ago. First using sonar equipment, then adding submersibles and magnatometers (sensitive metal detectors), and finally using satellites, scientists have begun to piece together a picture of the ocean's floor.

The harsh landscape of the abyssal plain was described earlier. No sunlight reaches these waters, but (surprisingly) many fish and plants thrive in this perpetual darkness. Forests of tubeworms and fern-like plants abound, especially near ocean vents. Fish, sharks, eels, shrimp, and crabs scurry past.

Scattered across the ocean floor lie vast mineral resources, manganese, magnesium, oil, copper, and zinc. The ocean water also contains valuable trace elements: gold, silver, bromine.

The belief is wrong. The deep ocean floor is covered mostly with sand, not mud. It is also a place filled with far more plant and animal life than scientists once believed possible. Yes, there are vast stretches of mud and vast plains devoid of life, but they are the exception, not the rule.

The ocean floor is a diverse and exciting place, one scientists would love to visit and study, if only they could stand the immense pressure of the deep ocean and if only they could easily get there.

— TOPICS FOR DISCUSSION AND PROJECTS

Here are activities, research topics, and discussion questions you can use to expand upon the key science concepts presented in this chapter.

Research and Discuss. The oceans were created billions of years ago. Since then, sea level has risen and fallen over the eons by as much as 800 feet. The ocean shapes have changed as the continents drifted. But have the ocean waters, themselves, stayed pretty much the same? Have the oceans changed because of human activity over the past 2,000 years? Over the past 300 years? Over the past fifty years? In what ways have the oceans changed?

An Activity. Build (or draw) a scale model that profiles the ocean floor of an ocean and specific place of your choosing from land down to the deep ocean floor. Research average depth for the shelf, the general angle of the rise and slope, and the depth of the deep ocean for the ocean and cross section you choose. What features will you include in your model? What bottom substance (sand, mud, etc.) will you put on your ocean floor? How would your model change if you picked another ocean and cross section? How would it stay the same?

Research and Discuss. How much do we know about the deep oceans and the things that live there? Compare what you find about the deep oceans to what you can find about the Moon and about Mars. How many pictures do you find of the floor of the deep ocean? How many pictures of the surface of the Moon and of Mars? Can you find the results of human visual studies? Of soil chemical analysis? Why do you think there is so much more information available about distant planets than about the abyssal plains of our own planet's deep oceans?

Research and Discuss. Research modern scientists' beliefs about the origin of, and early millennia of, our planet. Where did the mass that constitutes our planet come from? How did it gather together? Why did our planet initially form as a molten fireball when deep space is so cold? Why is Earth's core still molten? Where did the fire come from? When did Earth's atmosphere begin to form? When did the first water vapor erupt into that fragile atmosphere?

An Activity. Do a demonstration experiment to create a graphic image of how much water exists on Earth and how much of it is fresh water. You will need a good garden hose, a five-gallon bucket, a tablespoon, a teaspoon, several shallow cups, and a one-gallon container for this demonstration.

First, turn on the hose to simulate the first rains pouring water down on a new and barren Earth. Time how long it takes your hose to pour four gallons of water into the bucket. A hose with average pressure can flow at about four gallons per minute. If your hose poured water continuously every minute of every day at that same rate, how long would it take your hose to produce the 350 million cubic miles of water that exist on Earth?

Answer: a long time. 125 trillion years to be exact, or 7,500 times longer than the universe has existed. If you used *1 million* hoses, each pouring water at four gallons per minute, it would take them "only" 125 million years to produce the Earth's supply of water. That is a lot of water!

Now let's pretend that one gallon of water represents the Earth's entire supply of water. (Fill the one-gallon jug with water for this demonstration.) If that one gallon represents all water on Earth, how would you divide it to represent Earth's salt water and fresh water? Remove two tablespoons of water from your one-gallon jug and pour them into a shallow cup. The water still in the jug represents the Earth's supply of salt water. Those two tiny tablespoons represent all of the Earth's fresh water.

However, 80% of the Earth's fresh water is trapped in polar ice caps. How much is left for all human, plant, and animal uses on Earth—the amount in all rivers, lakes, streams, and ground water aquifers? Lift one and one-quarter teaspoons of water out of the cup and place these few drops in a second cup. That tiny amount represents all of the fresh water we and all other land-based life forms ever see or use. All of the rest of Earth's water is either locked in polar ice caps or is salty seawater.

Does that give you a sense of how big the oceans are? Does it make you think of how precious the planet's tiny fresh water supply is? Explain and defend your beliefs in a persuasive essay.

An Activity. Compare the four oceans. Prepare a chart showing the size (surface area), average depth, volume, surface temperature average and range, and salinity of each ocean. Add a list of significant bottom features (mountain ranges, sea mounts, trenches, and so on for each ocean). Finally, list the number of oceanographic research projects that have been conducted in each ocean. Which ocean was easiest to research? Which was hardest? Why?

An Activity. Create your own origin myth. Origin myths must explain how something began—a planet, an ocean, a people, some animal species, or even some specific characteristic of a specific group or species. Usually myths involve some superhuman being, God, or force. Usually there is some twist that makes the origination a surprise. What are your characters trying to do or get? What do they need? How do they finally get it?

SUGGESTED READING

Byath, Andrew, and Alastair Fothergit. *The Blue Planet: A Natural History of the Oceans.* New York: DK Publishers, 2001.

Collard, Sneed. *Deep Sea Floor.* Watertown, MA: Charlesbridge Publications, 2003.

Day, Trevor. *Oceans.* New York: Facts on File, 1999.

Elder, Danny, ed. *The Random House Atlas of the Oceans.* New York: Random House, 1998.

Erickson, Jon. *Marine Geology: Undersea Landforms and Life Forms.* New York: Facts on File, 1996.

Foder, R. V. *The Strange World of Deep Oceans.* Berkeley Heights, NJ: Enslow, 2001.

Groves, Don. *The Oceans: A Book of Questions and Answers.* New York: John Wiley, 1998.

Hanson, Neil. *The Curtain of the Sea.* New York: John Wiley, 1999.

Kent, Peter. *Hidden Under the Sea.* New York: Dutton Children's Books, 2001.

Leier, Manfred, ed. *World Atlas of the Oceans.* Tonawanda, NY: Firefly Books, 2001.

Markle, Sandra. *Pioneering Ocean Depths.* New York: Atheneum, 1995.

Oleksy, Walter. *Mapping the Seas.* New York: Franklin Watts, 2002.

Pernetta, John. *Guide to the Oceans.* Tonawanda, NY: Firefly Books, 2004.

Peterson, David, and Christine Peterson. *The Atlantic Ocean.* New York: Children's Press, 2001.

Sayre, April. *Ocean.* New York: Twenty-First Century Books, 1996.

Scholastic Staff, eds. *Scholastic Atlas of the Oceans.* New York: Scholastic, 2001.

Sonntag, Linda. *Atlas of the Oceans.* Brookfield, CT: Brookfield Press, 2001.

Stow, Keith. *Exploring Ocean Sciences.* New York: John Wiley, 1996.

Svarney, Thomas, and Pat Svarney. *The Handy Ocean Answer Book.* New York: Gale Research, 2000.

Swanson, Diane. *Safari Beneath the Sea.* Vancouver, British Columbia, Canada: Whitecap Books, 1997.

—— SUGGESTED READING FOR TEACHERS

Ballard, Robert. *Eternal Darkness*. Princeton, NJ: Princeton University Press, 2000.

Corfield, R. M. *The Silent Landscape*. Washington, DC: Joseph Henry Press, 2001.

Earle, Sylvia. *Atlas of the Deep Oceans*. Washington, DC: National Geographic Society, 2001.

Erickson, Jon. *Plate Tectonics: Unraveling the Mysteries of Earth*. New York: Facts on File, 2001.

Murray, John, ed. *Sea Coast Reader*. New York: Lyons Press, 1999.

Prager, Ellen. *The Oceans*. New York: McGraw-Hill, 2000.

Seon, Manley. *The Oceans: A Treasury of the Sea World*. Garden City, NY: Doubleday, 1997.

Shepard, Francis. *Geologic Oceanography*. New York: Crane and Russak, 1987.

Stevenson, Robert, and Frank Talbot. *Oceans: The Illustrated Library of the Earth*. Emmaus, PA: Rodale Press, 1996.

Waters, John. *Deep Sea Vents*. New York: Cobblehill Books, 1997.

2 .... Why the Sea Is Salty

——— MYTHS ABOUT WHY THE SEA IS SALTY

Rivers and lakes are filled with fresh water. Rain falls as fresh water. Clouds that bring rain are filled with fresh water that rose from the Earth's surface as evaporation—most of which came from the ocean. Springs bubble from mountain glades as fresh water. Yet these each flow into the sea and become salt water. Even polar ice and icebergs melt as fresh water and pour into the ocean. So why is ocean water salty? How did it first become salty? Where did the salt come from?

There are 350 million cubic miles of water on the surface of the Earth (or in near-surface groundwater aquifers). Only 3% of it is fresh. Eighty percent of that small amount of fresh water is locked into the polar ice caps. Only 0.6% of the world's water is available to sustain life and agriculture on this planet, and most of that is hidden in ground water aquifers. Humans and human activities require fresh water. Without fresh water, we will die. Yet only one-half of one percent of the world's water supply is available for our use. Thus, ancient cultures felt that they needed to explain why the sea is salty and thus useless to humans as a water source.

Your blood is salty—almost as salty as the oceans. So are your tears. Eighty percent of your body is water that, like the oceans, is salty. Where does this salt come from? Why must we drink fresh water and still have bodies made up of salt water?

Myths from more than eighty countries try to explain the saltiness of the ocean. A few say that tears created the ocean and that the ocean's salt is the salt from those tears. Most explain this ocean phenomenon by creating some magical device that creates on demand until ordered to stop. While being misused by someone who has stolen the device, it begins to create salt, but this time it does not stop and fills the oceans with salt. One of these myths is presented in this chapter. This German myth is typical of this group and features a brave maiden, a mean ogre of a man, magical beings that help the maiden, a wondrously magical object, and cunning treachery by the villain.

"HOW THE SEA BECAME SALTY," A MYTH FROM GERMANY

Long ago the wide rolling sea lapped at the toes of a town that hugged the rocky shore. The sea was as blue as a kingfisher's wing and each drop of sparkling seawater tasted as sweet as that from the purest mountain spring.

Behind the town rose a small hill with one small house perched at its top. Across a small valley rose a tall hill with a magnificent, tall house sprawled across its peak. In the tall house lived a tall, lean man who hoarded his cellars full of gold and silver and stuffed his pantry with puddings and pies and peaches and cream.

In the little house lived a little woman with her fifteen children. They had no money at all and their kitchen was bare except for two cobwebs and a stack of empty dishes.

"Will we have a New Year's feast this year?" the children asked.

The little woman shook her head. "There is nothing to eat but dreams and nothing in my pockets but holes.

"Can't we ask our uncle in the tall house to help us?" asked Yeta, the oldest of the children.

"Oh, no," answered the woman. "My brother was mean as a boy and he is meaner as a man."

Still, Yeta said there was no harm in asking. She wrapped her shawl about her and skipped down the small hill and up the tall hill.

"Go away," rumbled the voice of her uncle when Yeta knocked.

"But, it's me, Uncle," said Yeta.

"So?" growled the uncle.

"New Years is coming and I was hoping you would give us something so we can have a New Year's feast."

"Why should I?"

"Because you are kind?" answered Yeta.

"I am not!"

"Then because you feel sorry for us?"

"I do not. I never asked my sister to have all those . . . children.

I never asked her to waste her money on food and clothes. So I don't see why I should give you even one crumb just because it's New Years."

Yeta nodded. "Mother said you would say that." She sighed and shrugged. "Well, happy New Year, Uncle." And she turned to leave.

"Wait," ordered the uncle with a disgusted huff. He rummaged through a cupboard and handed her a small green bottle half-filled with water and a lumpy paper bag holding a small mound of over-dried bacon. "There. And don't ever bother me again!" And he slammed the door.

Yeta started for home. "At least this is . . . *something,*" she muttered.

As Yeta descended through the thick pine trees that curled around the tall hill, she heard a polite "Ahem!" and turned to see an old woman sitting on a stump. "Could I trouble you for a bite to eat and a drop to drink?"

Yeta gazed at the bottle and bag and then at the old woman. "It's supposed to be our New Year's feast . . . but how can I refuse to help an old lady?"

The old lady gulped the water and thoughtfully munched the dried bacon. "You deserve better for your feast. Do you have a good memory?"

"I have an *excellent* memory," Yeta replied and then, to prove it, spouted the names of her fourteen brothers and sisters first in order by age and then in alphabetical order. "Why, I can remember the exact dates of things that happened last year and the year before . . ." she continued.

"Good enough," the old woman interrupted. "Now remember *this.* Behind the two tallest trees in the darkest part of the forest is a small hole. Inside live seven tiny sisters. They are about to starve and would love the rest of this dried bacon."

"But it's *supposed* to be our New Year's feast . . ."

"The sisters will reward you. But accept only their silver churn."

"Their churn?" asked Yeta.

"Their *silver* churn! And remember, once you have it, wish for whatever you want, but say, 'Please stop churn, stop' to stop it." And before Yeta could say "but . . ." or "what? . . ." the old woman was gone. The word "remember" lingered in the air behind her.

Yeta found the darkest part of the forest and the two tallest trees. Sure enough, behind them was a small hole. From inside Yeta heard the sisters moaning about their hunger.

"Ahem . . ." she said. "I have some dried bacon."

Seven hands reached from the hole and snatched the bag. A contented sigh and furious lip smacking rose from the hole. Then a voice asked, "What can we give you in return? Gold?"

"I'd like your churn." Then Yeta muttered, "Whatever that is."

WONDERS OF THE SEA

"Our *churn*?!"

"Your *silver* churn."

Gnashing and wailing rose from the hole. Then, after a deep sigh from all seven sisters, out popped a small silver churn, hardly bigger than Yeta's hand. The churn looked like a miniature butter churn. Yeta shrugged, called "Thank you," and started for home wondering how her mother and fourteen brothers and sisters could have a New Year's feast with just a silver churn to place on the table.

"I'm surprised my brother gave you something this nice . . ." started Yeta's mother, once Yeta reached the small house on the small hill.

"Actually, he didn't. See, there was this old woman, and the seven sisters in a hole behind the tall trees . . ."

"Yes, yes," sighed her mother, turning away and not listening at all as she worried about how to feed her family. "I just wish we had a nice slab of meat for dinner."

Instantly the churn began to shake, to vibrate, to . . . well, churn. It hummed and buzzed. The top popped off and out flew a dozen steaks, a rump roast, a whole side of beef that bowled over one of the smaller children, a mutton leg, and an entire pig that squealed and oinked as it tumbled into a corner.

"My goodness!" cried the little woman.

"Hooray!" cried the children.

"That's enough!" screamed the little woman. And Yeta remembered. She smiled and said, "Please stop churn, stop."

The churn grew quiet and no more meat flew out.

Yeta thought, softly stroking her chin. Then she smiled and said, "I think some green beans would be nice with dinner."

Nothing happened.

She nodded and though again. "I *wish* we had green beans." Popping, shaking, buzzing, and humming began, and out flew green beans. Dozens of beans, hundreds of beans, mounds of beans, hills of beans.

"Enough!" cried the little woman.

"Please stop churn, stop!" said Yeta and all returned to quiet.

The family stared at their new treasure and knew they would never want for food again.

"My brother gave this to you?" asked the little woman.

"Actually, no, mother. There was an old woman and the two tallest trees and the seven sisters in a hole and they wanted the dried bacon . . ."

"Yes, yes," answered her mother, who had turned away, not listening at all as she dreamed of the feasts she would make with her new magic churn.

Soon the tall, lean, mean brother heard of the good fortune of his sister and came to visit. He heard about the churn from one of the smallest children and vowed to steal it. But when he asked to hold it and look at it more closely, Yeta snatched it up and said, "No, Uncle. You may not. It is ours."

The uncle cursed and muttered. Then he spun on his heel and stomped out.

Exactly one month later, on a bright afternoon with fleecy puffs of perfect clouds rolling above, Yeta sat on the harbor rocks watching the tall ships sail in and sail out.

One ship pulled up near her, tied ropes to some pilings, and stretched a gangplank to the shore. A tall, lean man in a long tattered coat and with a top hat pulled low over his eyes started down that gangplank, his steps so slow and feeble that Yeta feared he'd never make it to shore. He held a handkerchief to his face as he wept.

Yeta ran to the gangplank and asked how she could help.

"We are starving—all forty of us on this ship," the man sobbed. "But we were robbed by pirates and have no money. If only we had some food . . ."

"Wait right here!" said Yeta. "I can make you plenty of food."

She ran home and returned with the churn. But before she could say a word, the man snatched the churn, pushed Yeta down, ran up the gangplank, and the ship was away. The man flung off his top hat and tattered coat and there stood her uncle, laughing wildly from the railing with the churn raised in his hand.

Below decks at dinnertime, the captain said, "We have no salt for our dinner. You claim that is a magic churn and can make anything. Let's see it make the salt for our table."

The rough, tough sailors all crossed their tatooed arms, glared at the uncle, and chuckled in a pirate-ish sounding way, "Arrrr, Arrr, Arrrrr!" that were really muttered threats about what they'd do when he failed.

"Easy," sneered the uncle, snapping his fingers in the captain's face.

"I wish for salt," said the uncle. The churn whined and sputtered. It vibrated and hummed. And out poured salt. The cabin filled with salt. Salt spilled into the cargo hold and mounded upon the deck.

"Enough!" bellowed the captain. "Make it stop."

"Stop!" shouted the uncle. But salt continued to pour forth, climbing up the masts and rigging. "I *wish* you to stop!" screamed the uncle.

"Stop it or we'll sink!" cried the Captain, as he madly scraped salt over the side.

"Stop, I said," yelled the uncle. "Stop! Stop! STOP!"

But salt continued to erupt from the churn. The ship sank and all on board drowned. The churn settled into the soft sand at the bottom of the sea where there was no one to say, "Please stop churn, stop!" So the churn has continued to churn out salt from that day to this.

And that is why the sea is salty.

THE SCIENCE OF SEA SALT

The following beliefs are either directly stated or strongly implied in the presented myth. Here is what modern science knows about the aspects of the seas explained by each belief.

··

BELIEF: The oceans were originally fresh.

This belief is probably true—at least partly true. When the first clouds formed on this planet billions of years ago and began to rain, that rain was fresh water. It was that fresh water that initially spilled into the dry basins that would become oceans. It probably carried some minerals in the form of salts that the tumbling water scraped from the land (as rivers do even today). But those first rivers likely flowed with very little salt—only a few parts-per-thousand (ppt) of salt.* So the first oceans were certainly much less salty than modern oceans—if not actually fresh.

However, as soon as water began to fill the first ocean basins, two things began. The first was evaporation. As still happens, surface water slowly evaporated into the atmosphere. Most of this evaporation happened over the oceans. But evaporation pulls pure water (H_2O) into the atmosphere. All traces of salt were left behind to build up in the oceans. As water continued to evaporate from the ocean surface, the oceans grew ever saltier.

Second, volcanoes and vents continued to spew their eruptions of gas, water vapor, and lava. But some of those eruptions now occurred under water. This vent water was salty and pumped massive amounts of salt into the fledgling oceans. This "juvenile" water still spurts and steams into the oceans at ocean vents, undersea volcanoes, and along mid-ocean ridges, and it still pumps new salt into the oceans as it does. The salinity of the early oceans likely increased rapidly because of the direct in-

---

*Scientists measure many pollutants and trace elements in parts-per-million [ppm]. Out of every one million parts, how many parts is this thing I am measuring? But there is so much salt in the ocean, it is easier to measure parts-per-thousand [ppt] of salt. Ocean salinity is the only thing scientists measure in parts-per-thousand. Modern oceans range from just under 30 to over 35 ppt salinity, and they average around 33 ppt.

flux of juvenile water. Long before life evolved, the oceans were likely at about the same salinity levels they are at today.

BELIEF: Ocean was made salty all at once.

The myth makes it sound as if the ocean became salty in one catastrophic day. That certainly isn't true. Ocean salts built up over millennia and eons to reach their current levels.

Now the oceans' salinity levels have stabilized. They are no longer changing. They have reached what scientists call *equilibrium*. The amount of salt that falls out of the ocean's water to the ocean floor each year as salt crystals and in the shells of some plankton just equals the amount of salt that flows into the oceans from rivers and undersea vents.

There are also more than 4,000 factories around the world that pull salt water out of the ocean and change it into fresh water. Most are located in desert regions of the Middle East where rain and other fresh water sources are scarce. They use several different methods to draw the salt out of seawater. But all of them produce fresh water and a thick, salty brine that is toxic to oceanic and land plants and animals.

BELIEF: Fresh water has no salt.

Almost all water has some salt dissolved in it. Only evaporation water in nature is pure water (H_2O) and has no salt. Put a pan of fresh tap water on the stove and boil it all away. The white crust that remains in the pan is salt that had been dissolved in the water. If the water flowing in rivers and lakes really was "fresh," then the oceans would not be salty.

Lakes stay relatively fresh because river water, carrying some salt, flows out of them and keeps the lake from growing more and more salty. The oceans grew salty because they have no way to get rid of the salt that flowed in and slowly built up to their current salinity levels. The same thing happens in lakes if they have no outflowing river. Great Salt Lake in Utah and the Salton Sea in California are two American examples of such salty lakes.

Where do rivers get their salt? Minerals leech out of the ground and rocks as water gurgles past. Rocks break down as they are tumbled by flowing rivers. These minerals dissolve in the water as salts. The belief is wrong. All surface "fresh" water has some salt in it.

BELIEF: All oceans have the same salinity.

First, what do we mean when we say *salinity*? Salinity is a measure of the amount of salt dissolved in the oceans. But what do we mean when we say *salt*?

Table salt is sodium chloride—one atom of sodium (a metal) bonded with one atom of chlorine (a base). But a salt is any chemical compound made of one metal and one base. Seawater contains many mineral salts. Certainly sodium chloride is the most abundant of them. But seawater also contains magnesium chloride, calcium chloride, sodium sulfate (sodium combined with sulfur), calcium sulfate, magnesium sulfate, and calcium carbonate (calcium bonded with carbon). In addition there are traces (tiny amounts) of almost all of the other elements. That's why seawater has a distinctive taste and smell—noticeably different from a glass of tap water with table salt added.

The Dead Sea along the border of Israel is the saltiest body of water on Earth at over 100 ppt salinity. Its water is toxic to all plants and animals because it is so salty. California's Salton Sea has a salinity of around 80 ppt. A few species of shrimp and grass have adapted to this high salinity level and thrive in it.

The oceans vary from around 28 ppt salinity near shore, where fresh water pours in to dilute ocean water, to more than 35 ppt in some mid-ocean areas. Estuaries range from 3 or 4 ppt at their river end to around 24 ppt where they empty into the ocean. The salinity of estuaries also varies some with the tides. They are saltier at high tide when ocean water has flowed in and less salty at low tide when more of the salty ocean water has flowed back out.

Salinity does vary from ocean to ocean and from place to place within each of the oceans. However, that variation is small (only 7 or 8 ppt) so that almost all ocean water is near 33 ppt salt.

— TOPICS FOR DISCUSSION AND PROJECTS

Here are activities, research topics, and discussion questions you can use to expand upon the key science concepts presented in this chapter.

Research and Discuss. Is the ocean salinity changing? How long have scientists been measuring ocean salinity? Have their measurements changed over that time period? Do the ever-increasing amounts of waste that humans throw and pump into the oceans affect salinity? What would happen to life in the ocean if salinity increased to 60 ppt or decreased to 10 ppt? What would happen to coral reefs? To plankton? To large game fish?

Has ocean salinity changed a significant amount over the past 100 million years? How do scientists know? What clues do they look for and use to construct a picture of the ancient oceans? (Hint: Search the library and internet under the heading "Geological Oceanography.")

Research and Discuss. What is salt? Commonly, we think of salt as table salt. Table salt is one specific salt, sodium chloride (one atom of sodium bonded to one atom of chlorine. Its chemical abbreviation is NaCl. Is that the only kind of salt? What is the definition of a salt? How many salts are there? How many different kinds of salt are in ocean water? (Seawater contains other salts besides table salt, as well as eighty other chemicals, including gold and silver.) Why do we only think of sodium chloride when we think of salt?

Research and Discuss. Research the chemistry and biology of an estuary. What is an estuary? How would you define an estuary? Because of its salt content, ocean water is toxic to fresh water fish. Fresh water, because it lacks salt, is toxic to ocean fish. The sloshing, churning, mixing waters of an estuary form a transition zone, a buffer between fresh and salt water ecosystems.

An estuary contains a magnificently productive and diverse ecosystem of its own. Estuaries are nature's ocean nurseries, essential elements in the global aquatic ecosystem. Many of the species that live in estuaries are unique to estuaries—existing nowhere else on Earth. Biomass production in a healthy estuary exceeds even that for the most dense jungle.

That's all good, right? The problem is that most of world's biggest cities are tucked along estuaries: New York, Philadelphia, Baltimore, Washington, Los Angeles, San Francisco, Tampa, Houston, Seattle, Vancouver, Tokyo, London, and so on. More shipping and industrial activity is crowded along the shores of estuaries than anywhere else on Earth. Vast tracts of the marshes, reeds, and mud flats along the shores of American estuaries (essential to the health and productivity of the estuary) have been filled in for offices, factories, salt evaporation ponds, and housing. The fragile and essential estuarine ecosystems have been bombarded by a heavier load of human-generated pollution than have any other ecosystems on the planet.

Pick one major American estuary and research the environmental health of that estuary. What problems from pollution, dredging, and landfill operations plague that ecosystem? How have the fisheries in that estuary changed over the past 100 years? Have they expanded or diminished? What is being done to protect the estuary? What else could be done?

An Activity. Pick a small American estuary to research—one with only one in-flowing river. Where does it stop being a river and start being an estuary? Why? Draw a map of the estuary from upstream of the beginning of the estuary to the ocean. Research salinity levels and mark them on your map. Make a list of the major plankton and other sea plants that live and grow in the estuary. What fish migrate through the estuary? What fish live in the estuary? Mark industrial plants, commercial activities, and cities that have been placed along the estuary's shore. What problems does this estuary suffer from? What actions are local governmental agencies taking to solve them?

An Activity. Make a gallon of salt water at the same salinity as ocean water (35 ppt of salt). First, do the math. How many tablespoons of salt will you need to add to a gallon of fresh water to create ocean salt water? There are 16 tablespoons in a cup and 16 cups in a gallon. That's 256 tablespoons in a gallon. For every 1,000 parts (tablespoons in this case) of fresh water you will need to add 35 parts (tablespoons) of salt.

Your gallon of water only has 256 parts (tablespoons) of water, which is a tiny bit over one quarter of a thousand. So you must add a tiny bit more than one quarter of the 35 parts of salt you would need to turn 1,000 parts of fresh water into ocean water. That means your recipe for ocean salt water will be one gallon of water and nine tablespoons of salt (35 ppt ÷ 4 ≈ 9 tablespoons of salt). Use common table salt for this experiment.

Mix the water and table salt until all of the salt has dissolved. Now taste your ocean water. Does it taste salty? Does it taste like ocean water?

Your answers are probably "yes" to the first question and "no" to the second. But why no? What makes tap water plus salt different from seawater? What is added to tap water that is not present in ocean water? How many salts and minerals are in ocean water that aren't in either table salt or tap water?

Finally, set your salt water aside on a counter or table. Do you detect any changes in it after one day? After a week? Does some of the salt precipitate out and settle on the bottom? Does its flavor change? Does that give you any insights as to why ocean water stays salty?

An Activity. Let's make salt. How do salt companies make salt? How does nature do it? The answer to both questions is evaporation. Research evaporation. What is it? Why does it happen? How does it happen?

One important characteristic of evaporation is that pure water (H_2O) evaporates and leaves all impurities and additives behind. If salt water evaporates, the water evaporates and leaves the salt behind.

Place a thin layer of seawater in a metal baking pan. Pour some of your gallon of salt water from the earlier activity into a second pan. Set both of them out in the Sun and let them evaporate. The white crust left behind is salt. Taste it. Does it taste like table salt? What is the difference between the crust left in the two pans? If you don't live near the coast and can't get a jar of actual sea water, use only the salt water you made earlier.

You have made salt through evaporation. Research the companies that produce salt in the United States and the processes they use for making salt. Is their process similar to or different from yours?

An Activity. Let's make fresh water out of salt water. You have already seen that the salt dissolved in water stays in solution and won't precipitate out on its own. You have also seen that when water evaporates, it

FIGURE 2.1 · Experiment Set Up for Saltwater Evaporator

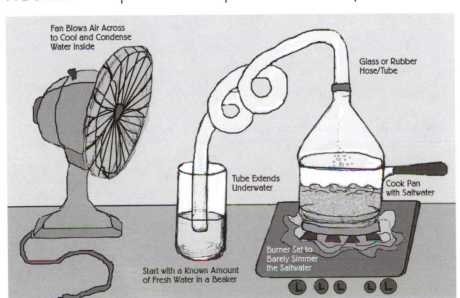

Fan Blows Air Across to Cool and Condense Water Inside

Glass or Rubber Hose/Tube

Tube Extends Underwater

Cook Pan with Saltwater

Start with a Known Amount of Fresh Water in a Beaker

Burner Set to Barely Simmer the Saltwater

leaves its salt content behind. Can you use this information to create a system that will turn salt water back into fresh water?

Use some of the salt water you created earlier to try a fresh water production experiment. Place this salt water in a glass chemistry lab beaker or in a small metal pan. Fabricate a loose cover over this pan to capture the steam you produce and to allow it to condense into water droplets. The diagram shows you a common set-up for this experiment.

Place your saltwater pan on a burner and heat the water almost to a simmer, but do not allow the water to actually boil. Allow most of the water to evaporate.

Watch to make sure that the water vapor (steam) you produce condenses back into water droplets and drips into a beaker or cup. Turn off the burner and allow the remaining salt water to cool.

Taste the water from the collection cup. Does it taste fresh? Now taste the remaining salt water. Is it saltier than when you started? Why?

Research commercial companies that convert salt water into fresh. How do they do it? Why don't they rely on evaporation as you did? Was it difficult for you to collect all of the steam you created and to condense it into water? Do you think some of the fresh water (steam) you created escaped into the air?

SUGGESTED READING

Alder, David. *Our Amazing Oceans.* New York: Troll, 1999.

Berger, Melvin, and Gilda Berger. *The Blue Planet.* New York: Scholastic, 2001.

Conkright, Margarita. *World Ocean Atlas, 2002.* Washington, DC: National Oceanic Atmospheric Administration, 2002.

Day, Trevor. *Oceans.* New York: Facts on File, 1999.

Diane Publishing Company Staff, eds. *World Ocean Atlas: Salinity.* Washington, DC: Diane Publishing Company, 1998.

Elder, Danny, ed. *The Random House Atlas of the Oceans.* New York: Random House, 1998.

Kerwood, Robin. *The Sea.* Milwaukee, WI: Gareth Stevens Publisher, 1998.

Lambert, David. *Kingfisher Young People's Book of the Ocean.* New York: Kingfisher Books, 1997.

Mamayen, G. *Temperature-Salinity Analysis of the World Ocean Water.* San Francisco: Elsevier Science, 1998.

Sayre, April. *Ocean.* New York: Twenty-First Century Books, 1996.

Scholastic Staff, eds. *Scholastic Atlas of the Oceans.* New York: Scholastic, 2001.

Svarney, Thomas, and Pat Svarney. *The Handy Ocean Answer Book.* New York: Gale Research, 2000.

—— SUGGESTED READING FOR TEACHERS

Bohnecke, Gunther. *Temperature, Salinity, and Density of Surface Water of the Atlantic Ocean, 1978–1998.* New York: Ashgate, 2002.

Brandt, Alan, ed. *Double Diffusion Convection.* New York: American Geophysical Union, 1996.

Leuwickli, Andre. *Salinity.* Philadelphia: Kluwer Academic Press, 2002.

Lewis, Edward. *Water Budget of the Arctic Ocean.* Philadelphia: Kluwer Academic Press, 2000.

Millero, Frank. *Chemical Oceanography.* Chicago: CRC Press, 1999.

Seon, Manley. *The Oceans: A Treasury of the Sea World.* Garden City, NY: Doubleday, 1997.

Wallace, William. *Development of the Chlorinity-Salinity Concept in Oceanography.* San Francisco: Elsevier Science, 1994.

3 .... Ocean Tides

———————— MYTHS ABOUT OCEAN TIDES

The flowing in and flowing out of the tides dictates the coming and going of ships and of coastal activity. It defines the rhythm of life along the coasts.

Not so around a lake. Not so in tropical waters where the tide only rises a foot or two from low tide to high. In these places, the tide creeps in and out, its changes unnoticeable from minute to minute. Most people in the tropics ignore the tide in the conduct of their daily lives.

But in the upper latitude, bands around the globe (between 30 and 70 degrees north and south latitude) tides control coastal activity. In northern bays, tides roar in and out to the extreme danger of the unwary. In these latitudes, the tide can rise twenty to forty feet from low to high, rising so fast, you can literally watch the tide roll in.

Ships and boats have great difficulty maneuvering against these tidal currents and must wait for the tide to turn in their favor before attempting to sail. Beyond 30 degrees north or south latitude, the tide is critically important to sailors, fishermen, and coastal wanderers and becomes more important as you travel toward 70 degrees of latitude.

Yet tides were a perplexing mystery for early civilizations. Tides seem to hold no relationship to any other known phenomena—not to wind, not to storms, not to season, not to temperature, not even to time of day since the tides shift from high tide to low and back to high in twelve hours and twenty-six minutes. Tide height varies from one high tide to the next, seeming to follow no pattern at all. No, the tides could only be explained as a mysterious phenomenon controlled by some unseen and unknown force. It was the perfect topic for myths.

Virtually all myths attempting to explain the existence and pattern of the tides rely on the intervention of supernatural beings and forces. In Scandinavia, the god Thor is said to cause the tides with his mighty breath, breathing in and out twice a day.

In a Thai myth, a giant sea dragon causes the tides as it swishes its tail from side to side. The dragon is a league in length with a hairy tail and shaggy legs. Fish are boiled by the blast of its breath. When it rises to the surface, the whole ocean surges (tsunamis). When it flies through the air, monstrous storms (typhoons) spin from its wings. When it lies content in its undersea castle and gently swishes its tail, the tides roll back and forth across the ocean.

In a Japanese myth the Sea God holds two lustrous pearls. When the god raises one, the tide comes in. When he raises the other, the tide goes out. In a Chinese myth, two warring groups of gods cause the tides as their battle rages back and forth. The story presented below comes from the Tsimshiam tribe of the Pacific Northwest and relies on the clever trickster, Raven, to start the motion of the tides.

"HOW RAVEN MADE THE TIDES," A MYTH FROM THE PACIFIC NORTHWEST

A long time ago, the old people say, the tide did not come in or go out. The ocean stayed very high along the shore and would not budge. The clams and crabs and seaweed and other good things to eat stayed hidden under the deep waters. The people were often hungry.

"This is not the way it should be," said Raven. "I must find out what is so wrong." He put on his blanket of black feathers and flew along the coast, following the line of the shore. At last he came to the house of a very old woman. Raven peaked in the window and saw that this old woman sat in a chair and held the tide line tight in her hands. As long as she held it, the tide would stay high and would never flow out.

Raven knew he would have to trick the old woman into letting go of the tide. Raven walked into the woman's house and contentedly sighed. The old woman sat, the tide line firmly gripped in her hands, and she suspiciously watched Raven.

Raven sat down across from her and patted his belly. "Ahhhhh," he said. "Those clams were wonderful to eat."

"What clams?" demanded the old woman.

But Raven did not answer her. Instead he patted his stomach and said, "Ahhhh, it was so easy to pick them up and I have eaten as much as I can eat."

"That can't be so," said the old woman, trying to look past Raven to see out her door and down to the ocean. But Raven blocked the entrance as he continued to smile and pat his stomach.

The old woman's brow furrowed and her mouth twitched back and forth. Finally, she stood and leaned past raven to see if it was true that her tide line had sagged and exposed the sea creatures to Raven's greedy appetite.

As the old woman awkwardly leaned, still gripping the tide line in both hands, Raven pushed her so that she tumbled out the door. As she fell, Raven threw sand and dust in her eyes so that she was blinded. She let go of the tide line and the tide rushed out, exposing clams and crabs and seaweed and other good things to eat.

Raven dashed out and gathered clams. He gathered as many as he could carry and ate until he could eat no more. Other people, too, rushed out to gather clams and crabs.

But the old woman, still blinded, groped across the sand until she felt the tide line. She clutched it in her hands and dragged it back into her house and sat back in her chair. The people had to climb onto rocks to escape the quickly rising tide.

Raven went back to the old woman's house. She said, "Raven, it is not right that you played such a cruel trick on me. Heal my eyes."

Raven answered, "It is not right that you hold the tide so high all the time. The people will starve. I will heal your eyes if you let go of the tide."

"I can not. It is my task to sit in my chair and hold the tide. It is what I do."

Raven gazed at her chair and blinked his eyes, and then he smiled. "May I borrow your chair for one day?"

"You tricked me before . . ."

"This is not a trick," he interrupted. "I will heal your eyes if you let me take your chair for one day."

Raven washed out her eyes and she could see again. For one day the old woman stood and held the tide line. Then Raven returned and placed her chair facing the ocean. On the bottom of the chair he had built long rockers.

Now as the old woman sat and held the tide line she could rock back and forth. When she rocked forth, closer to the ocean, the tide rolled out. When she rocked back, the tide rushed in.

And the old woman still sits and slowly rocks back and forth, still contentedly gripping the tide line. So it is that the tide rolls in and out twice each day giving the people a chance to gather food from the beach—all because Raven was clever enough to make it so.

THE SCIENCE OF OCEAN TIDES

The following beliefs are either directly stated or strongly implied in the presented myth. Here is what modern science knows about the aspects of the seas explained by each belief.

BELIEF: Tides are caused by action of the gods.

Gravity causes the tides. The gravitational attraction of the Moon pulls on the Earth. It pulls on every rock, tree, and person on Earth. However, that force isn't strong enough to move solid objects. The stronger gravity of the Earth holds us where we are. However, liquids flow. Liquid molecules are not bound to a single shape and form. So the ocean facing the Moon bulges a little bit toward the Moon as ocean water responds to the Moon's gravitational pull.

As the Earth rotates, this oceanic bulge rotates so that it always faces toward the Moon. This bulge causes the ocean surface level to rise and fall, creating the tides. Even though tides happen everywhere in the ocean, they are only noticeable along the coast where they can be measured against the land that doesn't move.

Because the Moon is also moving (traveling around the Earth once every 28 days), it takes 24 hours and 52 minutes for any point on the Earth to revolve back directly underneath the Moon. (The 52 minutes represents how far the Moon traveled around the Earth in one 24-hour period.) That is why the tides are keyed to a cycle of 24 hours and 52 minutes to change from high tide to low, to high, to low, and back to high tide again. When the Moon is overhead, high tide occurs. When the Moon is above the exact opposite side of the Earth a second high tide occurs—but this high tide isn't as high as the one when the Moon is overhead because the Moon is farther away and its effect is masked by the bulk of the Earth.

Every twenty-four hours and fifty-two minutes each point along the coast has a higher high tide (Moon overhead), a lower high tide (Moon on opposite side of Earth), and two low tides (when the Moon has traveled a quarter way around the Earth).

However, the Moon isn't the only heavenly body that exerts a gravitational pull on the ocean waters. So does the massive Sun. Because the Sun is 93 million miles away instead of the Moon's quarter of a million miles, the Sun's gravitational pull is much weaker. But it is still noticeable in the tides.

FIGURE 3.1 • The Earth, Moon, Sun, and the Tidal Bulge

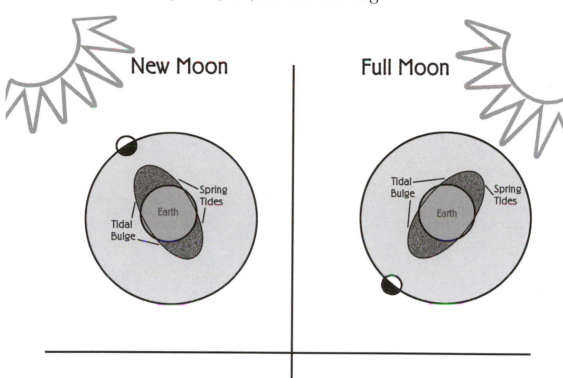

New Moon

Spring
Tides

Earth

Tidal
Bulge

Full Moon

Tidal
Bulge

Spring
Tides

Earth

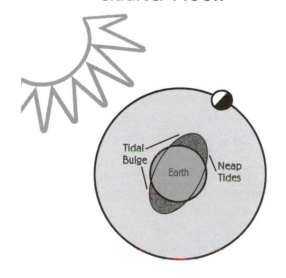

Quarter Moon

Tidal
Bulge

Earth

Neap
Tides

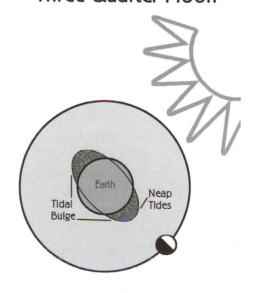

Three Quarter Moon

Earth

Neap
Tides

Tidal
Bulge

The Moon circles the Earth once every twenty-eight days. Twice during that twenty-eight-day cycle the Moon and the Sun are exactly aligned and tug on the ocean waters in the same direction. High tides on these days are higher than high tides on any other days and are called *spring tides* (although spring tides have nothing to do with the season of spring). One week later, halfway in between the spring tides and when the Moon and Sun are at right angles to each other and so pull the ocean in different directions, the coasts record their lowest high tide of the twenty-eight-day cycle. This lower high tide is called a *neap* tide.

Spring tide, neap tide, higher high, lower high tide, low tide—the tides roll in and out, beating to the rhythm of the seas and the heavens, like a pulse beat for the living oceans.

The myth is wrong. Neither gods nor Raven nor some old woman cause or control the tides. Simple interplanetary gravity controls our tides.

· ·

BELIEF: Tides are the same everywhere.

Tides are actually even *more* complicated than described above. The latitude of a spot on Earth also affects the height of the tides so that—even at the same time on the same day—different spots along the coast experience different tidal heights. The height of the tide measures the difference between higher high tide and low tide. Near the equator the tide may only rise and fall a foot between high and low. It's barely noticeable.

The farther away from the equator you go, the greater the height of the tides. In the band that stretches between 50 degrees and 65 degrees of latitude you find the highest tides on Earth. In Canada's Bay of Fundy tides can rise as much as forty-three feet from low tide to high. During the peak tidal flood, the tide there rises at the amazing rate of a foot every four or five minutes! You can literally watch the tide come in. Alaska's Cook Inlet has tides almost as great. Above that latitude, tidal height begins to shrink again.

Finally, moving high pressure and low pressure air masses affect tide levels. High pressure atmospheric systems, like a heavy hand, push down on the water and slightly flatten the tides. When low pressure storms roll in, bringing wind and high waves, they also bring higher tides. Why? Low atmospheric pressure acts like a partial vacuum and sucks the tide water a little higher. The term *storm surge* refers to the higher than expected surge of water at high tide during a storm. Storm surges combined with powerful storm-generated waves create most of the coastal damage and flooding during storms.

Again, the common belief is wrong. Tidal height varies widely from spot to spot and from day to day. For something that rocks back and forth like clockwork, the tides are actually very complex things!

BELIEF: Ocean currents are created by gods.

Currents, like tides, represent the movement of water within the oceans. Currents are giant rivers flowing through the oceans. The earliest sailors quickly discovered the existence of currents and learned to route themselves to take advantage of these rivers within the ocean. Sailing along ocean currents is like sailing downstream instead of upstream. Currents were known and charted, but rarely appeared in mythic story—maybe because only sailors experienced currents, maybe because ocean currents were not potentially dangerous.

Two questions arise when talk turns to currents: *Where* are the ocean currents, and *why* are there currents in the ocean?

Spin a glass that is half full of water and you will notice that the water right next to the glass sides spins faster than the water nearer to the center. Friction between the glass and the water right next to the glass drags the water along, but not as fast as the solid glass. Similarly, moving water tugs at the water next to it and drags it along—but not as fast.

The Earth spins on its axis and, just like the glass, drags ocean water with it. That dragging sets up currents in the oceans that cause water to circulate around the ocean basins. In the Northern Hemisphere, those currents tend to spin clockwise in great *gyres* around ocean basins. In the Southern Hemisphere they spin counterclockwise. Oceanographers call the force that drives these currents in those specific directions the *Coriolis force*.

The Gulf Stream is part of the North Atlantic gyre. The cold California Current that flows south along the west coast of North America is part of the North Pacific gyre.

In 1990 a load of 60,000 Nike tennis shoes was spilled from a cargo ship into the ocean off of the Alaska coast. In late 1990 and early 1991 some of those shoes washed up along the Oregon and California coasts. In 1993 some washed up in Hawaii. In 1996 a few found their way to Japan. In 1997 the few shoes remaining afloat began to show up along

FIGURE 3.2 • Major Ocean Surface Currents

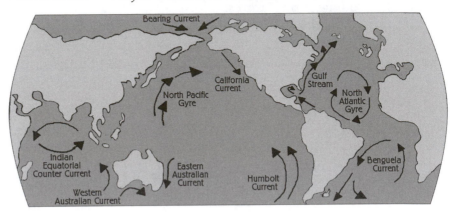

the Canadian coast. In seven years those shoes drifted almost 25,000 miles around the North Pacific, following the current of the North Pacific gyre!

The stated belief is wrong. The continuous spinning of the Earth causes surface ocean currents.

But the spin of the Earth is not the only thing that drives ocean currents. Temperature differences can create ocean currents. Cold water is denser (heavier) than warm water. Bitter-cold water flowing off of polar ice sheets is heavier than surrounding ocean waters. The cold water sinks and starts a vertical current that circulates through each of the oceans. Surface water is drawn north toward the poles where it chills, sinks, and flows along the ocean bottom back toward the equator.

Major ocean surface currents flow in great gyres around the ocean basins driven by Coriolis forces. Vertical currents sink down at the poles and up nearer to the equator, flowing toward the equator on the bottom and toward the poles on the surface. Combine this with the tides flowing back and forth, and ocean water is forever in motion.

— TOPICS FOR DISCUSSION AND PROJECTS

Here are activities, research topics, and discussion questions you can use to expand upon the key science concepts presented in this chapter.

Research and Discuss. Tides exist all over the world. Think for a minute about the advantages and disadvantages, the plusses and dangers, of having tides. What do tides *do*? In what ways are tides useful and beneficial? When can they be destructive and dangerous? What do tides expose when they flow out and cover up when they flow back in? What is a "storm surge" (something that happens at high tide during a major coastal storm). Research the effects of tides and decided if you think they are a net good or bad thing for humans.

Research and Discuss. Tides create the intertidal zone and tide pools along the shore. The intertidal zone is that area on the beach and coastal rocks that lies between the low tide and high tide marks. Research what lives in this very narrow and specific area. Certainly clams, mussels, shore crabs, urchins, starfish, and sea anemones. But what else depends on the intertidal zone for survival?

How many of those species are unique to the intertidal zone? What is a tide pool? What lives in a tide pool? Where are they found?

An Activity. Gravity creates the tides—primarily the Moon's gravitational pull and, to a lesser extent, the Sun's. When those two heavenly bodies are in line and pull on the Earth's oceans in the same direction, Earth experiences its highest tides (spring tides). Draw a chart to illustrate when spring tide and neap tide events happen within the cycle of the Moon.

First, draw a schematic chart showing the Earth, the Moon circling it, and the distant Sun. Use a dotted line to show the Moon's circular orbit around the Earth. On that orbit, draw the Moon in four places: where it is when it is a full Moon (draw a full Moon), when it is a new Moon (draw a shaded—darkened—Moon), and the two times when it is a quarter Moon (draw the Moon half in shadow, half in sunlight).

Think about the Moon's position for each of these four Moon phases. Where would the Moon have to be so that we, on Earth, can see the entire side that faces the Sun? (We call that situation a full Moon.) Where would the Moon have to be if we on Earth can see none of the side of the Moon that faces the Sun? (We call that a new Moon.) Label each of the four Moon phases on your schematic—Full Moon, New Moon, and Quarter Moon.

When are the Moon and Sun in alignment? At a quarter Moon? New Moon? Full Moon? Does your chart show that spring tides occur when we see either a new or a full Moon and that the highest tide will happen during a new Moon?

Watching the phases of the Moon is an easy way to predict the height of future high tides.

An Activity. On a map of the Atlantic Ocean, map the historical sailing routes used by sailing ships between Europe and North America. On the same map overlay the major surface currents. Now compare. Did sailors sail with the currents? Why?

Research and map the famous "triangle route" that sailing ships took between Europe, Africa, and America in the seventeenth to early nineteenth centuries. What cargoes did those ships carry on each leg of this triangle? Why did they always travel clockwise around this triangle? (Hint: Think gyre.) Did the direction of the prevailing current influence why African slaves were off-loaded and sold in America instead of in Europe?

An Activity. Many myths as well as the science discussion above mention that currents move heat. On a world map, mark arrows showing the direction of major north and south flowing surface currents north of the equator. Color the arrow blue if the current flows from a polar zone toward the tropics. Color the arrow red if that current flows from an equatorial area toward the poles.

Pick three pairs of coastal cities. Each pair should sit at approximately the same latitude. One city in each pair must sit on a coast bathed by a warm current (red arrow) and the other must sit on a coast bathed by a cold current (blue arrow). For each city in each pair, research and list average annual temperature, average high and low temperatures, and annual rainfall. Within each pair, which city has the higher average annual temperature. Which has the higher (warmer) average annual low? Which city in each pair is, overall, warmer? Which is wetter? What does that tell you about how major surface ocean currents move heat and water?

An Activity. Create a graph to show how tidal range varies with latitude. Pick six North American ports and research high and low tide ranges for each. Prepare a graph showing latitude on one axis and tidal height on the other for these six port locations. Can you find places that have the lowest tides in the Western Hemisphere? The highest? Do you see a pattern that relates average tidal height to latitude? Explain.

SUGGESTED READING

Arnold, David. *Tides and Currents*. Seattle, WA: Sea Ocean Books, 1997.

Berger, Melvin, and Gilda Berger. *The Blue Planet: Part 4. Tidal Seas*. New York: Scholastic, 2001.

Jacobs, Marian, and Nancy Ellwood. *Why Do Oceans Have Tides?* Greenville, NC: Joyner Library, 1999.

Kerwood, Robin. *The Sea.* Milwaukee, WI: Gareth Stevens Publisher, 1998.

Kingland, Rosemary. *Savage Seas.* New York: TV Books, 1999.

Kunzin, Robert. *The Restless Sea.* New York: Norton, 1999.

Lambert, David. *Kingfisher Young People's Book of the Ocean.* New York: Kingfisher Books, 1997.

McKeone, Richard. *Tides and Ocean Currents.* New York: Franklin Watts, 2002.

Neumann, Gerhard. *Ocean Currents.* Boston: Elsevier Science, 2003.

O'Mara, Annie. *Oceans.* Mankato, MN: Bridgestone Books, 2000.

Rogers, Daniel. *Waves, Tides and Currents.* New York: Franklin Watts, 1999.

Sylvester, Doug. *Oceans Alive: Water, Waves & Tides.* Braintree, MA: Rainbow Horizon Books, 2001.

Wiegel, Robert. *Waves, Tides, Currents and Beaches.* Berkeley, CA: Berkeley Books, 1989.

—— SUGGESTED READING FOR TEACHERS

Arnold, David. *Tide Tables and High and Low Water Predictions*. Washington, DC: U.S. Coast and Geodetic Survey, 2004.

Blaylock, James. *Winter Tides*. New York: Ace Books, 2002.

Clemons, Elizabeth. *Waves, Tides and Currents*. New York: Alfred A. Knopf, 1997.

Halversen, Catherine. *Ocean Currents*. Berkeley: University of California Press, 2001.

Marchuk, G. I., and B. Kagan. *Dynamics of Ocean Tides*. Philadelphia: Kluwer Academic Press, 1989.

Thruman, Harold. *Essentials of Oceanography*. Upper Saddle River, NJ: Prentice Hall, 1999.

Walton, Smith. *The Seas in Motion: Waves, Tides, Currents and How They Work*. Seattle: University of Washington Press, 1997.

Wust, Georg. *Atlas of the Stratification and Circulation of the Atlantic Ocean*. Burlington, VT: Ashgate Publishing, 1996.

4 ⸱⸱⸱⸱⸱⸱⸱⸱⸱⸱⸱⸱⸱⸱⸱⸱⸱⸱⸱⸱⸱⸱⸱⸱⸱ Ocean Waves

———————— MYTHS ABOUT OCEAN WAVES

Playful beach waves are the joy of surfers and of children scampering along the sand. However, waves also sink ships, drown beach goers, destroy buildings, smash coastal bluffs, and terrify anyone who ventures onto the ocean in rickety wooden boats. Waves can roll for a thousand miles across the oceans, unaffected by the length of their travel, and then roar as they explode on coastal rocks.

Waves are powerful and dynamic. So they were often thought of as animate beings. Many early myths related waves to horses. Waves were thought to be alive and were often called children of the sea god. Poseidon, the Greek sea god, is often pictured riding a chariot pulled by foaming wave in the shape of horses. The white crest of waves is often described in South American myths as being the mane of a great sea horse. Their sea gods rode foaming horses across the ocean. In Celtic myths, the horse of Manannan drove the waves toward shore.

The existence of waves, especially large storm waves, was usually explained as being the result of an angry sea god. Poseidon created waves with his trident. For the Inuit people of Alaska, the God Aulanerk created waves with his voice when he grew angry and yelled.

In this Filipino myth (itself a creation myth of the water-came-first variety), waves are called forth and driven by an angry sea god. The myth's intrigue rides in a simple bird who, like other cleaver tricksters, is able to manipulate and maneuver the gods into doing her bidding.

"THE BATTLE OF SEA AND SKY," A MYTH
FROM THE PHILIPPINES

When time began, there was only the blue sky, the flat, smooth sea, and a single black bird. Because there was no land yet, the bird had no choice but to fly continuously through the air, day after day. When her wings grew tired, she stretched them open as wide as she could, letting the wind carry her for long distances.

One afternoon the bird grew so tired she could scarcely open her wings to glide with the wind. She knew that some day soon she would grow too tired to fly and would sink into the ocean and drown. She had to think of a way to rest her weary wings or she would die.

In those days, the sky hung very low, almost scraping the sea. The bird gazed up at sky and down at sea and wondered, "How can I use the sky and the sea to create a place where I can rest?"

She thought for several days before a plan crept into her mind. Perhaps if sea and sky were jealous of each other, they would move apart and create a place between them where she could rest.

The bird swooped low to the sea and said, "The sky tells me that you are a worthless body of salty water and that you do nothing important. The sky says you can't even help me fly as it does."

The sea hissed, "The life in me runs deeper than the shallow sky can ever imagine. There is a world under my liquid surface much richer than anything in the sky."

The bird twittered up to the sky and whispered, "The sea says you are thin and worthless. The sea says that you can't even hold me up and that you make me flap my wings as hard as I can just to keep from drowning."

The sky was angered by these words. "I stretch all the way to the heavens," cried the sky. "I rise above and over all. From his lowly view, the sea sees nothing and knows nothing."

The bird dove back down to the glassy ocean surface. "The sky says that you are a good-for-nothing and that you can't keep me safe or let me rest and that you will probably drown me one day."

The sea was enraged. "The sky dared say such words?! I'll drown the sky with my water!"

The bird nervously asked, "*Drown* the sky? How?"

"I'll build my waters into towering mountains I call waves. I'll smash them against the sky and soak him with my wetness."

"You will?" gulped the bird. "But *I'm* up here too!"

The waters turned black and began to churn. The sea lifted her waters from ripples into roaring waves, rising higher and higher. From each wave the sea flung her spray back and forth as they smashed together. Towering waves rose toward the sky, spraying foam across the sky's face. Mountainous, angry waves raced across

the water, frothy foam lashing from each crest. The deep roar of
the rushing waters rumbled as loud as thunder.

"Take *that,* you lying, worthless, sky!" roared the sea.

"*This* isn't what I wanted," squawked the bird, fluttering her
tired wings with all her might to dodge the waves and spraying
water and to keep from being waterlogged and drowned. It seemed
the sea would surely drown the very sky and her with it.

The sky swiftly pulled itself up out of reach. But the sea drove
its towering waves higher to reach toward the heavens, soaking the
sky with its salty wetness.

And now the sky filled with anger and bellowed for revenge.
The sky darkened with boiling, black clouds. Lightning bolts
blasted down to strike the ocean, scalding the seawater where they
struck. Rocks and boulders rained down from the blackened
heights of heaven, shattering the towering waves when they struck.

The bird desperately flitted left and right, up and down, trying
to stay out of harm's way. Rocks, waves, lightning, and spray
ripped through the air from all directions. "What have I done?"
she cried. "This is worse than ever. I'll be killed instead of saved!"

The fierce battle between sea and sky raged for days. The little
bird was convinced that she was about to die. She closed her eyes
and waited, terrified, to be smashed, sizzled, or drowned.

Then, as suddenly as it began, everything stopped. Cautiously,
the bird sailed through the clearing sky that was now quiet, bright,
and blue. She gazed down at a calm, smooth sea. But she also saw
rock formations jutting above the ocean's surface that hadn't been
there before.

As soon as she was sure the sea wasn't going to rise up in anger
and throw her vicious waves against these rock intruders, the bird
drifted lower and lightly touched her feet to the highest crag. "At
last," she sighed. "A place to rest."

As far as she could see, rock formations rose from the sea. Some
were large, some only tiny outcroppings barely above the waves. As
they grew and as they settled, they became the islands of the
Philippine archipelago, which, even today, includes more than
7,000 islands.

But the sea *did* hurl her waves against the land—endlessly
smashing at their shore. And she still does, for she has never for-
given the sky and is still trying to tear down the land that he created.

THE SCIENCE OF OCEAN WAVES

The following beliefs are either directly stated or strongly implied in the presented myth. Here is what modern science knows about the aspects of the seas explained by each belief.

. . . .
BELIEF: Waves are caused by gods.

The myth says that a sea god (or at least the sea, itself) creates waves. The story is wrong.

Wind creates waves. Period. Every wave in every ocean is created by wind. Wind blows across still water and the friction between moving air and still water causes some of the wind's energy to transfer into the water, bunching the water into tiny ripples. As the wind continues to blow, it gives energy to these waves in two ways. First, wind swirls in behind each wave and blows on it as if the wave were a sail. Second, continued friction between wind and water imparts more energy into each wave.

Long, steady winds create neat, regular trains of waves—each long wave following behind the one in front, like the coupled freight cars of a train, as they march across the ocean. Wave trains can roll undiminished for thousands of miles across the ocean. When one wave train meets another train traveling in a different direction (caused by a wind blowing over a different part of the ocean), then the ocean surface grows choppy.

The size of each wave in a wave train is determined by the strength of the wind that created it and by the distance over which the wind blew. The stronger the wind and the longer it blows, the higher the waves it will create.

There are several terms that are used to describe waves.

Crest. The top or highest point of a wave.

Trough. The low dip between two wave crests.

Wave Height. The vertical distance from trough to crest.

Wave Length. The horizontal distance from one wave crest to the next.

Period. The length of time for two subsequent wave crests to pass the same point.

FIGURE 4.1 · A Wave Profile

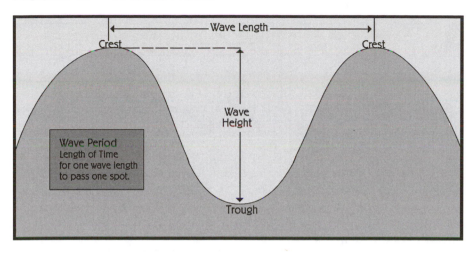

The tallest wave ever measured rose 112 feet from trough to crest. That monster wave—the height of a twelve-story building—was measured by the USS *Ramapo* during a 1933 South Pacific typhoon.

The belief and the myth are wrong. Ironically, it is not the sea, but the sky and its wind that create waves.

BELIEF: Waves are moving water.

Water looks like it surges forward and moves with a wave. But it doesn't. Currents and tides move water. Waves are moving trains of energy. Wave *energy* moves; the *water* stays in one place. Actually, water particles move in a circle as a wave passes, ending up exactly where they started. Each water particle receives the waves energy, moves in a vertical circle, and passes the energy to the next molecule.

Wave energy doesn't travel just on the surface of the ocean. A wave has depth. It is a moving wall of energy with depth and width. Anyone who has snorkeled or gone scuba diving knows that you can be thirty feet under the surface and still feel the passing of each wave. But the wave is less powerful down there than it is at the surface. Most of a wave's energy rides close to the surface and its energy diminishes with depth.

When a particle of water first feels an approaching wave, it is sucked back and down into the trough ahead of the wave. It continues moving back but starts moving up as the wave crest approaches. The particle rides up to the top of its circle at the crest of the wave and finally moves for-

FIGURE 4.2 · Water Motion in a Wave

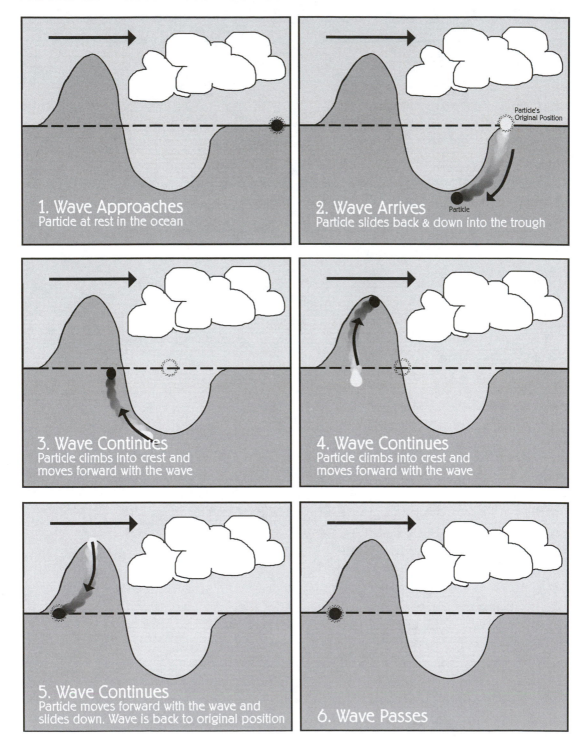

1. **Wave Approaches**
Particle at rest in the ocean

2. **Wave Arrives**
Particle slides back & down into the trough

Particle's Original Position

Particle

3. **Wave Continues**
Particle climbs into crest and moves forward with the wave

4. **Wave Continues**
Particle climbs into crest and moves forward with the wave

5. **Wave Continues**
Particle moves forward with the wave and slides down. Wave is back to original position

6. **Wave Passes**

FIGURE 4.3 • Waves are Moving Walls of Energy

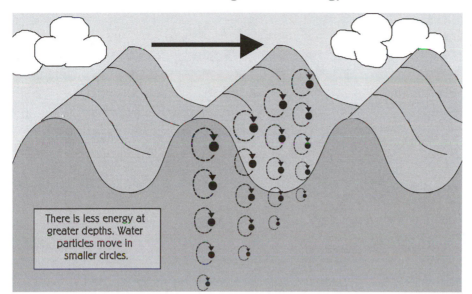

There is less energy at greater depths. Water particles move in smaller circles.

ward and down as the wave passes, returning to the spot where it started. The wave's energy has moved on. The particle of water is back at rest in the ocean—until the next wave arrives. These circles are biggest at the surface where the energy is greatest and decrease in size deeper and deeper under the surface as the wave's energy decreases.

Those who swim in the ocean have felt this motion. You are first pulled out toward an approaching wave, ride up the face of the wave, and are finally carried back toward the beach as the wave passes and moves on. The water carries you through that circular motion because it is moving through that same pattern itself.

But what happens when a wave reaches the beach? Why do they grow taller and break? Remember, waves are walls of energy traveling through the ocean, moving water particles in a circle as they pass. As the water grows shallow, a wave's energy begins to feel the bottom—to literally scrape along the sand and rocks of the ocean floor. The bottom of the wave begins to drag along the bottom, to lag behind the top. At this same time, energy in the bottom of the wave is forced up. That pushes the water higher and thus pushes the wave crest higher, making the wave grow taller.

Right at the beach, there is no new water to continue the circle motion of the water as a wave passes. The last water on the beach is sucked out into the bottom of the wave (water always starts its circle motion

FIGURE 4.4 · Waves Approaching the Beach

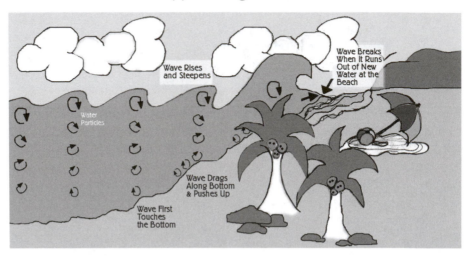

by moving down and back). The wave grows unstable as the water particles in the top of the wave try to complete their circle. They curl forward and start down. But there is no water there for them to settle into. The wave becomes top heavy and breaks in a beautiful and thunderous curl for surfers to ride and the rest of us to watch and enjoy from beach blankets.

Water does not advance with a passing wave. Waves are moving trains of energy. Each water molecule simply rolls in a neat circle as the wave passes. It is that circular motion that creates the trough and hump that we see and call a wave.

. . . .

BELIEF: Tsunamis and rogue waves are an expression of anger by the gods.

Tsunamis

A tsunami is a single, high-energy wave that travels at high speed through the ocean and can cause tremendous damage when it reaches shore. What causes tsunamis? Undersea earthquakes, landslides, and volcanoes can trigger a tsunami. Do they always? No, but they can. Tsunamis race outward like shock waves from one of these undersea disturbances at speeds of up to 600 miles per hour.

Tsunamis are rare. Only a handful happen each century. But the destructive power of a tsunami makes each one memorable. Tsunamis carry massive amount of energy and so stretch much deeper than regular waves. Common ocean waves typically reach twenty or thirty feet deep. The energy column of a tsunami can be hundreds of feet deep. Tsunamis are usually not noticeable in the open ocean to surface ships. On the surface, they feel like just another small wave.

But as tsunamis near the coast, they become the most dangerous waves on Earth. These waves are so deep that they start to feel the bottom and thus build higher often a half mile from shore. They can suck an entire bay's water out as the first part of water's circular motion through a wave. Tsunamis then grow to fifty—even 100—feet in height as friction against the sea floor begins to slow them down.

Tsunamis slam into the shore with thousands of tons of water hurtling onto shore at speeds of more than 100 miles an hour, destroying anything in their path. Entire towns can vanish as a tsunami roars through. Breaking tsunamis have picked up large ocean-going ships and dumped them miles inland. The word *tsunami* is Japanese for "large wave in harbor." Tsunami is an astounding understatement for these all-powerful, all-destructive monsters.

Are tsunamis predictable? Yes, because they only occur in response to a major seismic event along the ocean floor. Depending on the location and strength of that event, scientists can predict the direction, speed, and size of the tsunami the event could produce. However, it is extremely difficult to detect a tsunami until it approaches shore.

The largest tsunami ever recorded was created by the Krakatoa eruption of 1883. People heard that explosive volcanic eruption 3,000 miles away. The tsunami it created reached a height of 125 feet when it slammed into neighboring islands. It killed thousands and completely destroyed a dozen villages, leaving not even one stick to show where thriving communities had lived only minutes before.

On December 26, 2004 a massive undersea earthquake just off the north coast of Sumatra created a deadly tsunami that roared across the Indian Ocean at speeds of up to 550 mph. The earthquake measured 9.0 on the Richter scale and released energy equivalent to 32 billion tons of TNT—more than the total explosive power of all nuclear weapons on Earth.

The resulting tsunami reached heights of up to fifty feet as it approached shore. It struck, without warning, since tsunami warning nets do not exist in the Indian Ocean as they do in the Pacific. The tsunami struck along thousands of miles of shoreline in twelve countries and even raced 4,500 miles across the Indian Ocean to strike the eastern shore of Africa. Buildings, trees, even entire communities were flattened. Thriving coastal towns turned to a clutter of rubble in less than thirty seconds.

The death toll from this massive wave climbed to over 200,000. Its moment of thunderous destruction will affect the lives of local inhabitants for generations to come. Interesting, when the earthquake shifted massive amounts of the Earth's crust, it slightly changed the Earth's spin rate. Just as a spinning skater accelerates by tucking in her arms, the earthquake compacted the Earth's crust and increased the Earth's spin rate. As a result each day is now three-microseconds shorter than it was before the earthquake.

Rogue Waves

Rogue waves are giant waves that form in the ocean for no apparent reason. Towering above other waves, some rogue waves last only a few seconds before falling back into the sea. Sometimes rogues race as towering giants for miles across the open ocean, crushing ships and deep-sea oil platforms and terrorizing all who witness the wave and live to tell about it. Rogue waves are truly a bizarre phenomenon and seem most like random and capricious acts of the gods. People on land have often thought that rogue waves are the wild exaggerations of sailors.

But rogue waves are very real and, science has recently discovered, far more common than previously thought. Rogue waves have capsized large ocean-going freighters. Rogues have swept sunbathers off beaches when they were lying a dozen yards from the shoreline. Rogues have smashed and destroyed offshore oil platforms in the North Sea and in the Gulf of Mexico. Rogue waves are killers.

Modern chaos theory mathematicians have been able to model rogue waves in their computers. Using these computer model results, other scientists and engineers can now create and study rogue waves in large wave tanks.

Here is what they have found. When a sea or ocean has complex wave patterns traveling in different directions and at different speeds, at some point the energy from all those separate wave trains unites. Instead of the energy from one wave lifting water toward a wave crest, it is suddenly the energy from four or five—or ten—wave trains simultaneously doing the lifting. This jolt of extreme energy lifts water into towering monsters often ten times higher than any other wave for miles around.

The direction, period, and height of the individual wave trains will determine how long a rogue will last before collapsing back into the sea.

While rogue waves are now understandable, are created by the complex interactions of many wave trains (not by the gods), they are definitely not predictable. Rogue waves are one of the terrors of the deep every sailor must accept and prepare to meet.

— TOPICS FOR DISCUSSION AND PROJECTS

Here are activities, research topics, and discussion questions you can use to expand upon the key science concepts presented in this chapter.

Research and Discuss. Research beach waves. Why do they bend as they approach the coast and break parallel with shore? (Hint: remember that waves have depth and slow down as they drag along the bottom. The part of the wave in the shallowest water will start to slow first and will slow down the most.)

Where are the biggest waves along the east coast? Along the west coast? What time of year? What causes those waves to grow so big in these places and at these times?

Research and Discuss. Describe your experience on the beach with waves. Standing in thigh-deep water, have you first felt the water pull you out and down toward an incoming wave? Then did it lift you up the face of the wave and then throw you forward toward the beach as it broke? Is this the circular motion described earlier in action? Have you seen the top of a breaking wave actually curl in the water's attempt to complete its circular motion? Could you see the waves grow higher as they approached shore and the wave's energy was pushed up by the shallower water bottom?

An Activity. Conduct a wave making experiment. You will need a rectangular tub to use as your wave tank. The three- to five-foot-long (and two feet wide) plastic tubs used to mix cement are ideal. Fill your tub with six to eight inches of water.

Now let's make some waves. First, do it the way that nature does it. Kneel at one end of the tub and place your mouth just above the water and blow across the water toward the other end of the tub. Don't blow down onto the water. Blow parallel with the water's surface, across the water. Blow softly and steadily for three breaths. Then sit back and study the wave trains you have created. They will be little more than ripples, but they will be marching steadily toward the far end of the tub.

Once they reach that end they will bounce back toward you again. Notice that the waves don't move as straight lines. The ends tend to spread out in a circular pattern so that some of the wave energy hits the side of the tub and ricochets at an angle back across the tub. Soon tiny wave trains are bouncing left and right, back and forth, and you have a classic choppy ocean surface. It will be choppy because waves are colliding from many different directions.

Let the water calm again and repeat the experiment. This time blow harder. If possible, have two people blow side by side and in the same direction. A bigger wind should create bigger waves.

Now let's watch a single wave move across your ocean more carefully. Use a ping pong paddle or salad plate of about the same size. Insert your paddle vertically along one end of your wave tank so that the paddle's tip is about two inches deep in the water. Flick your wrist to move the paddle forward about three inches and lift it out of the water.

If you flick too hard, you will produce turbulence and lose most of your wave energy to chaotic motion. If you move too slowly, you will not produce a visible wave. Practice a few times and then let the water in your wave tank calm before conducting the actual experiment.

Watch the shape of your wave as it moves down the wave tank and begins to reflect off the sides and far end. Draw a top view of your waves when it was one-fourth, one-half, and three-quarters of the way down the tank.

Did it stay as a single wave or spread its energy to create several new waves in front of and behind it? Did it move as a straight line or did the ends curve and spread?

Let the water again return to calm and repeat the paddle experiment one more time. This time push the paddle forward, lift it out, and then quickly push the paddle back into the water along the wall of your wave tank and make a second wave as quickly as you can. Watch the two waves. Do they travel at the same speed? Do they hold the same shapes? Do they interact or move through the water independently? Notice how long the waves slosh back and forth. Water is very efficient at moving energy. Again draw simple top-view pictures of the progress and movement of your waves.

Contact a local university or research institute that has a real wave tank. Ask for pictures of their wave tank in action and descriptions of the kind of research projects they conduct in their wave tank. Visit the tank if you can and watch the tank in action. What do they learn from wave tank studies?

An Activity. How deep is a wave? Earlier science discussions said that waves are really moving walls of energy. Let's see if that's true. Make sure your wave tank has about six inches of water in it and that the water is still and calm. Use an eye dropper to slowly, carefully place three drops of red dye (red food coloring will do nicely) one above the other in the middle of your wave tank. Place the first dot just above the bottom. The second one should be directly above the first and in the middle of the water column. The third drop should be placed above the first two and barely under the surface.

Blow moderately from one end of the wave tank for three good breaths to create waves. Watch your three dots as these waves approach and pass.

Did the bottom one move at all? Could you see the circular pattern of the top drop's motion?

Wait for the water to calm and replace the dots if necessary. Blow harder and longer this time. What difference did you see in the motion of your three marker dots?

Research and Discuss. Research ship disappearances at sea. What are listed as the causes of disappearance? Many were likely due to storms. If so, storm conditions should be listed in the ship's information. Search for disappearances during clear skies and relatively calm seas. Were any of these disappearances suspected of being caused by rogue waves? Make a chart showing where rogue waves have been sited and where ship disappearances have occurred.

An Activity. Prepare a map showing the locations where tsunamis have struck shore over the past century. Research one of these tsunamis. What caused it? How far did the tsunami travel? How big did the tsunami wave grow at the shoreline? What damage did it do?

SUGGESTED READING

Bascom, Willard. *Waves and Beaches*. Garden City, NY: Anchor Press, 1996.

Berger, Melvin, and Gilda Berger. *What Makes an Ocean Wave?* New York: Scholastic Reference, 2001.

Kampion, Drew. *The Book of Waves*. Niwot, CO: Robert Rinehart Publishers, 1998.

Kehret, Ray. *Escaping Giant Waves*. New York: Simon & Schuster Books for Young Readers, 2003.

King, Andrew. *Tsunami*. San Diego: Lucent Books, 2001.

Littlefield, Cindy. *Awesome Ocean Science!* Charlotte, VT: Williamson Publishers, 2002.

Rogers, Daniel. *Waves, Tides and Currents*. New York: Franklin Watts, 1999.

Smith, Walter. *The Sea in Motion*. New York: T. Y. Crowell, 1998.

Souza, D. M. *Powerful Waves*. Minneapolis, MN: Carolrhoda Books, 2002.

Stern, Richard. *Tsunami!* New York: Norton, 1998.

Svarney, Thomas, and Pat Svarney. *The Handy Ocean Answer Book*. New York: Gale Research, 2000.

Sylvester, Doug. *Oceans Alive: Water, Waves & Tides*. Braintree, MA: Rainbow Horizon Books, 2001.

Thompson, Luke. *Tsunami*. New York: Children's Press, 2000.

Wiegel, Robert. *Waves, Tides, Currents and Beaches*. Berkeley, CA: Berkeley Books, 1999.

Young, I. R. *Atlas of the Oceans: Wind and Wave Climate*. Boston: Elsevier Science, 1996.

—— SUGGESTED READING FOR TEACHERS

Clemons, Elizabeth. *Waves, Tides and Currents*. New York: Alfred A. Knopf, 1997.

Dudly, Walter. *Tsunami!* Honolulu: University of Hawaii Press, 2001.

Komen, G. J. *Dynamics and Modeling of Ocean Waves*. Princeton, NJ: Princeton University Press, 2001.

Ochi, Michael. *Ocean Waves: The Stochastic Approach*. New York: Cambridge University Press, 1998.

Pedlosky, Joseph. *Waves in the Ocean and Atmosphere*. New York: Springer-Verlag, 2003.

Walton, Smith. *The Seas in Motion: Waves, Tides, Currents and How They Work*. Seattle: University of Washington Press, 1997.

Young, Ian. *Wind Generated Ocean Waves*. Boston: Elsevier Science, 1999.

Zim, Herbert. *Waves*. New York: William Morrow, 1997.

5 .... Ocean Storms

—————— MYTHS ABOUT OCEAN STORMS

Violent storms at sea have always lurked in the shadows of sailors' nightmares, hiding just over the horizon, waiting for the worst possible moment to pounce and to crush. Hurricanes, typhoons, whirlpools, water spouts. It seems nature outdid herself in providing a variety of deadly storms to throw at fools who tread upon her seas.

Fear of terrible sea storms led to myths that tried to explain those storms, to create order in their seemingly random acts of violence, and to fortify sailors so that they would dare to venture beyond the breakers again. All myths on the topic agree: Storms are the creations of angry gods.

The word *hurricane* comes from the Myan word *huraken*, the name of their god of storms. In the Atlantic Ocean, major cyclonic storms (storms that spin counterclockwise) that have winds over seventy-four miles per hour are called hurricanes. In the Pacific they are called typhoons. Typhon was an Asian mythic sea dragon, a vicious monster with a hundred dragon heads, whose wings darkened the sky, whose eyes flashed lightning bolts, whose scaly body was bigger than a mountain. The word *typhoon* comes from this monster that locals believed caused violent storms. Typhon worked his way into Greek mythology as a fierce monster and was the only being ever to defeat Zeus in one-on-one combat.

Hurricanes and typhoons plague the warm water reaches of the tropics. European sailors never encountered a hurricane until Columbus reached the new world, where his small fleets were pounded by hurricanes in 1494, 1495, and 1502.

Major ocean storms have changed the fate of nations and started wars. Twice Kublai Khan, the ruthless Mongol ruler of China, tried to invade Japan—once in 1274, once in 1281. Both invasion fleets were destroyed by chance typhoons as they tried to land the Chinese army on the Japanese coast. The grateful Japanese honored their stormy savior by giving the wind-driven storms the name *kamikaze*, meaning "divine wind."

A 1568 hurricane forced Englishman John Hawkings and his fleet to seek emergency shelter and repairs in the Spanish port of San Juan de Ulloa in the Gulf of Mexico. There, Spanish forces attacked the British, killing many and capturing the rest. The incident enraged the British government and precipitated an English-Spanish war.

Violent sea storms have killed countless thousands of sailors, driven fortunes of cargo and treasure to the ocean floor, and for thousands of years have made sailors afraid of the open ocean. Such fear needed to find a voice, and that voice came through myths. In a Japanese myth, a giant fish causes tsunamis and earthquakes. In a myth from Figi, tsunamis and typhoons are caused by men's attempt to fool and outwit a woman sea goddess. In a Chinese myth, a sea god is enraged when a scribe accompanying the king on his visit to the god sketches a portrait of the god. (The god had expressly forbidden being sketched.) The result was destruction and storm beyond measure.

The Indonesian myth that follows is typical of this group of myths in that it attributes sea storms to the vengeful whims of a god. This theme is wrapped around a moral tale in which the penitent and faithful are rewarded and those who lack proper reverence for the gods are squashed by the fearsome storms gods can so easily fling at frail mortals.

"The Queen of the South Sea," a Myth from Indonesia

Pak Sodin and his wife, Nadsura, squatted in the mud and wept. Puffs of gentle wind tugged the sleeves of his cotton shirt. The wind was the last teasing echo of the terrible storm (typhoon) that Ratu Loro Kidul, the Queen of the South Sea, had lashed across the land. Pak Sodin's fine rice field was now a muddy wasteland and their sturdy house no more than a twisted pile of broken sticks. Their buffaloes, like many of their friends and neighbors, had been swept away and killed.

"Ratu Loro Kidul hates us and wants to destroy our lives," cried Pak Sodin.

"What shall we do?" wailed Nadsura. "Where shall we live?"

For a long time, Pak stared silently at his ruined fields. "I cannot be a farmer now," he finally said. "The Queen of the South Sea has stolen our farm. But I have already spoken to the men who collect birds' nests from the caves in the high cliffs to sell. I will do that until I have enough money to rebuild the farm."

Nadsura gasped and trembled. "But husband, those cliffs tower above the raging sea. What of your fear of Ratu Loro Kidul?"

Pak answered, "I have no money to buy rice plants or buffaloes or even a hoe to work the land. I will make a peace offering to the Queen of the South Sea and pray that she grants me safety while I climb the jagged cliffs."

Early the next morning Pak Sodin saved out just enough grain and rice to feed his family for one day. All the rest of the rice that he had salvaged from the storm (it was only two coconut shell bowls full) he divided into two piles. One he painted red, the other he painted yellow so that even if his sacrifice was too small to be worthy of the Queen of the South Sea, at least it would be beautiful to see.

Wearing his finest cloth, Pak Sodin carried the two bowls of colored rice to the offering place, laying them down and offering prayers to the Queen of the South Sea just as the Sun rose above the ocean in the east.

Then Pak Sodin walked with the other men to the top of the cliffs. Along the path, he walked next to Nuk Rule, a rich and famous cliff climber. Nuk Rule's wife had prepared a lavish offering to Ratu Loro Kidul for her husband to leave on his way to the cliffs. In the offering basket Nuk Rule carried roasted chicken and pig, fried fish, mangoes, and bananas. Nuk reached into the basket and ripped off a chicken leg to munch while they walked.

"The storm did not hurt me at all," Nuk boasted as he tossed the chicken bones into the bushes and licked his fingers. "In fact, storms are good for me. They knock slippery moss off the cliff rocks. I'm glad we had a typhoon." His hand rummaged in the basket for a juicy mango.

Pak Sodin said, "But the storm killed many villagers and it ruined my farm. How can you be glad for such a thing?"

Nuk Rule paused for a moment, as if thinking. Then he shrugged and ripped off another piece of offering chicken. "Then there will be more birds' nests for me on the cliffs and more land for me in the village."

By the time they reached the cliffs, Nuk Rule had only banana skins and bones in his basket to leave on the offering mat for Ratu Loro Kidul.

Pak Sodin stood frozen with fear at the top of the cliffs. Jagged rocks reached straight down over a thousand feet and seemed to stretch to the bottom of the world. The ragged rocks at the surf line looked like hungry teeth waiting to rip poor Pak's body apart.

Each wave that crashed over those rocks shook the cliffs and rumbled like angry thunder.

"Don't look down," said Nuk Rule, beginning the climb down one of the hanging rope ladders that waved in the swirling winds. Where the ladders ended, long ropes had been secured into the cliff rocks. Climbers lowered themselves down the ropes and then swung left or right to reach a cave they would explore for sellable birds' nests.

At the bottom of the ladder—and still many hundreds of feet above the crashing waves and hungry looking rock teeth—Pak Sodin again hesitated. Fear of both the heights and of the wrath of the Queen of the South Sea froze his legs and his heart.

"Try a close-by cave so you won't have to swing very much," Nuk Rule said. "Maybe you'll be lucky." Then he sneered and laughed to show that he didn't believe what he had said and slid far down a rope to swing in great loops for a cave that had never been explored before.

Pak closed his eyes and whispered, "I must be brave and bring home birds' nests so Nadsura and my children will be able to eat." He grabbed a rope, slid down a few feet, and swung into the first cave he found.

Inside Pak blinked to adjust to the dark. The winds moaned and swirled. Pak thought he heard a voice say something about oysters. Pak looked and blinked but no one was there.

But again he heard the voice. "I left oysters for you Pak Sodin. They are a gift for your generous offering and for the trouble my storm caused."

Pak spun back toward the cave entrance and fell to his knees. "Great Ratu Loro Kidul?" he tried to say, but his voice was as dry and thin as rice straw.

"Don't let anyone else see them," the voice instructed. "They are just for you and your family."

In front of him where he knelt, Pak found six large oysters. He knew the voice had to be the Queen of the South Sea and he dared not disobey. He wrapped the oysters in his headband, climbed out of the cave, up the rope ladder, and ran toward home and his family, clutching the oysters to his chest.

Meanwhile, Nuk Rule found a promising cave but felt drowsy from his large meal and stretched out to nap. He awoke with a start when the crashing waves shook the cave and sent small rocks tumbling down its sides.

Outside the sky had darkened through deep green to vengeful black. The waves had risen into towering monsters that slammed against the cliff as if to tear it down. Clouds boiled thick and low as the wind howled and screeched.

"Glutton!" thundered a voice. "Why did you dare to eat my sacrificial offering?"

Nuk rushed to the cave entrance and grabbed for the rope. But a giant wave rose to smash against the cliff, erupting into a howling spray, and sent a torrent of water to tumble Nuk Rule back inside.

Nuk's wife raced to the cliff top and, fearing for her husband's life, called out, "Oh, great Ratu Loro Kidul, spare my husband. Please give us a reward as great as my husband's morning offering was to you."

"Granted," roared the Queen of the South Seas as she slammed a giant wave against the cliff. "He left me bones. So I will bring a storm that will leave you bones!"

Clouds boiled. Lightning exploded against the cliff. Rain fell in torrents and drove the people back toward shelter. A wave that looked as big and dark as a mountain roared across the ocean and exploded against the cliff.

Spray rose a thousand feet above the cliff's top and soaked everyone standing nearby. Water from that wave hit Nuk Rule like a sledgehammer and crushed him back against the cave's rock wall. Then the wave washed his broken body out to sea where it was squeezed by octopuses and devoured by sharks. His broken bones washed back in to litter the beach.

Breathless from his sprint home, Pak Sodin slid to his knees in front of his wife and children. "Look! A gift of oysters from the Queen of the South Sea for us to eat."

But when Pak pried open the oysters, he found a magnificent, lustrous pearl hidden in each.

Pak sold the pearls for a small fortune with which he rebuilt his farm and bought rice plants and buffaloes for himself and for his neighbors. He became a happy farmer, as rich in wealth as he was in generosity. For the rest of his life, Pak was especially generous in his offerings to the Queen of the South Seas. She, in return, steered her violent storms away from his village and happy farm.

THE SCIENCE OF OCEAN STORMS

The following beliefs are either directly stated or strongly implied in the presented myth. Here is what modern science knows about the aspects of the seas explained by each belief.

BELIEF: Storms are not created by natural forces,
but by supernatural forces (gods).

The same forces that create storms on land cause storms at sea. The Earth spins, causing the atmosphere to swirl and flow. Solar heat strikes the tropics with greater intensity than it does the high latitude regions. The heat differences cause colder air to sink and warmer air to rise. Warm, wet air masses collide with cold air masses dipping low from frigid polar regions. And—*whamo!*—a violent storm explodes across the landscape (or seascape). Rain pounds down. Winds wail and roar from high pressure to low. Lightning snakes to the ground along the frontal boundary between air masses.

If the storm occurs over land, trees dip and sway. Streets flood. Tree limbs break and crash down. If it happens over oceans, waves rise and steepen into threatening giants. Winds blow wave crests into foaming spray that lashes at ships and exposed skin. Towering waves may make ordinary frontal storms seem more threatening at sea, but the storms themselves are no different than land storms.

However, there are other, special storms that only form over warm tropical oceans and are the real ship killers. The land has tornadoes and blizzards. The oceans have cyclones. In the Atlantic they are called *hurricanes*; in the western Pacific they're called *typhoons*.

What causes hurricanes and typhoons? The Sun burns down most fiercely in the tropics, heating the tropical ocean waters and turning tropical oceans into heat engines—engines that fuel and drive these greatest of all storms. Warm tropical surface waters heat the air and stuff it with moisture. Hot air rises. The Earth's Coriolis forces make the rising air column begin to spin. Rising air cools and its moisture condenses into clouds.

The ocean's heat continues to fuel and drive the developing storm, pumping more heat and energy into the gathering, spinning clouds, driving the winds higher and higher so that they growl and snarl like predators. The storm grows and spreads, spinning harder, massive cloud banks swirling around a central clear eye and looking from the top like a spiral galaxy. Lightning flashes glow through the clouds looking like giant photo flashes.

Hurricanes continue to grow and strengthen as long as they travel over warm water. They begin to weaken when they travel over land or over cool water and are no longer fed the heat energy they crave from the tropical ocean. Hurricanes carry that heat energy farther north as they weaken and die. Tropical storms redistribute heat away from the tropics and toward mid-latitudes. Natural forces, not vengeful sea gods, create storms and use them to rebalance the Earth's heat.

BELIEF: Ocean storms are bad and evil.

Many societies have thought that violent ocean storms represent chaos and something going wrong in nature. The truth is that storms are the natural order of things and are efficient ways for nature to redistribute heat and energy and to rebalance the atmosphere and oceans. Far from holding evil intent, storms serve the valuable service of spreading tropical summer heat into the higher latitudes to the benefit of the world's ecosystem.

Certainly ocean storms are dangerous to humans caught in their mighty clutches and are worth avoiding if possible, but the world's ecosystem depends on storms to maintain global heat, energy, and water balances. Storms—even violent hurricanes—are neither bad nor evil.

BELIEF: Ocean storms can be controlled by sacrifice and prayer in an attempt to appease the gods.

Storms cannot be controlled. They cannot be dispersed or reduced through human action. But they can be anticipated and forecasted through improved data collection and mathematical modeling. Weather and storm forecasting have made tremendous advances over the past thirty years. Once-a-day weather balloons from the 1970s have been replaced by a network of satellites that continuously monitor surface and atmospheric conditions twenty-four hours a day. Early numerical models of storm movement have been replaced by advanced computer simulation models.

Storm data collection is regularly augmented by specialized planes that fly into building storms to gather detailed data on winds, atmospheric pressure, and storm conditions. Land-, airplane-, and ship-based radar systems probe ocean storms for sheer forces and changing wind conditions. Ocean buoys collect and transmit sea surface temperatures and sea condition changes.

Advanced computers using state-of-the-art chaos theory models compile this mass of data in order to forecast storm tracks and storm formation. Still, storm forecasting is difficult. Accurate predictions are elusive. The atmosphere is a complex system that can change radically from minute and random changes in any of a number of base conditions. Storms and weather are virtually impossible to anticipate with certainty. All forecasters can say is what is *likely* to happen and how likely it is. *Probabilities*, not absolute and certain forecasts, are the best modern technology can offer. The probability that the forecasters' best guess for storm track and strength is right decreases rapidly as the period of the forecast stretches beyond a few days into the future.

BELIEF: The ocean controls weather on land.

In the myth, storms coming from the ocean dictate weather over land. Is this what normally happens? To a large extent, yes. Most evaporation occurs over the oceans—and especially the tropical ocean. Water vapor content helps determine how one air mass will interact with another as well as the cloud and rain amounts that an air mass will produce once it flows over land. The tropical oceans warm the air and produce the warm air masses that flow north into the mid-latitudes. Those warm, tropical air masses produce much of the rain that falls on the eastern United States.

Similarly, arctic cold fronts, chilled by the polar ice caps and frigid Arctic Ocean waters, produce the storms that dump bitter-cold winter rain and snow across the west and northern states.

Ocean waters strongly influence weather along all coasts by affecting air temperature near the shore. Ocean waters store solar energy and control global heat circulation, and thus strongly influence all global weather. Ocean currents also shift massive amounts of heat and change atmospheric circulation, climate, and weather patterns.

The power of ocean currents to affect weather can be seen in the phenomena called *el niño* and *la niña*. These conditions are produced by small shifts in the surface temperature of the eastern tropical Pacific Ocean. However, those temperature shifts of a few degrees either up or down from the norm radically change precipitation patterns all over the world. Prolonged droughts and severe floods have been tracked back to *el niños* and *la niñas* as have prolonged hot spells and unseasonable cold snaps.

What happens in the oceans does change and control what happens with weather and climate on land.

— TOPICS FOR DISCUSSION AND PROJECTS

Here are activities, research topics, and discussion questions you can use to expand upon the key science concepts presented in this chapter.

Research and Discuss. Has global warming over the past fifty years changed the patterns of, frequency of, season of, and/or intensity of major oceanic storms? Research hurricane and typhoon statistics to support your belief. Are there more big storms now than there were fifty years ago? One hundred years ago? Do you think that global warming should affect hurricane production and strength? Why? How?

What is a hurricane? Create your own definition for these giant storms and compare yours to what is in the dictionary and to meteorologists' definitions.

An Activity. Collect clippings and reports that allow you to track the origin point and paths of recent hurricanes and typhoons. Plot these storm tracks on a world map. Search for patterns. Do major storms tend to be created in the same area of the ocean? Do they tend to follow the same tracks? In what months do they occur? Why do they occur in those months? Why do they have a "season" at all? (Hint: What do hurricanes need? When can they get it from the oceans most easily?)

An Activity. Make a chart of the fifteen most costly and the fifteen most deadly hurricanes. Compare these statistics to a second chart showing the ten most costly and ten most deadly typhoons in recorded history. How do these storms compare with the damage and deaths caused by other types of storms? Research and prepare similar statistics for blizzards, tornadoes, and rain-induced floods.

An Activity. Interview a local weather person. Ask him or her what creates major land- and ocean-based storms and to explain how ocean storms grow, where they get their energy, how they act, and why they act that way. Do ocean storms form for the same reasons as land storms?

Ask the weather person to describe available weather forecasting and storm forecasting technology, equipment, and methods. Which technology is most reliable? Which do they use in their daily work?

Research and Discuss. Two ocean temperature phenomena have become famous. Their names are *el niño* and *la niña*. In one of these, surface temperatures in the eastern equatorial Pacific Ocean rise above normal. In the other, these same surface temperatures sink below normal. Both conditions create weather havoc around the world. Research *el niños* and *la niñas*. What happens in each? Why does it happen? What effect does each have on weather around the world? What has been the impact on human life? Make a chart showing the years in which *el niños* and *la niñas* have occurred during the past fifty years and summarize the weather effects of each and their impact on human life.

An Activity. Set up a weather station at your school to monitor and record temperature, humidity, barometric pressure, and wind direction and speed. Which of these data points best indicate an approaching storm? Can you predict storms by using any of these indicators? How far in the future can you predict the weather using your weather station?

SUGGESTED READING

Allaby, Michael. *Hurricane.* New York: Facts on File, 2003.

Berger, Melvin, and Gilda Berger. *Do Tornadoes Really Twist?* New York: Scholastic, 2000.

Garbuny, Carole. *Nature's Fury: Eyewitness Reports.* New York: Scholastic Reference, 2000.

Green, Jen. *Hurricanes and Typhoons.* Brookfield, CT: Copper Beech Books, 1998.

Hicolson, Cynthia. *Hurricane!* Tonawanda, NY: Kids Can Press, 2002.

Jennings, Terry. *Hurricane.* New York: Thameside Press, 2000.

Kingland, Rosemary. *Savage Seas.* New York: TV Books, 1999.

Lakin, Patricia. *Hurricane!* Brookfield, CT: Millbrook Press, 2000.

Morgan, Sally. *Hurricanes.* Brookfield, CT: Copper Beech Books, 2002.

Murray, Peter. *Hurricane.* Chanhassen, MN: Child World Press, 1999.

Sheels, Bob. *Hurricane Watch.* New York: Vintage Books, 2003.

Simon, Seymore. *Hurricanes.* New York: HarperCollins, 2003.

Williams, Theresa. *The Secret of Hurricanes.* San Francisco, CA: Cage Publications, 2002.

—— SUGGESTED READING FOR TEACHERS

Bradford, Marlene, ed. *Natural Disasters*. Pasadena, CA: Salem Press, 2001.

Davies, Pete. *Inside the Hurricane*. New York: Henry Holt, 2000.

Longshore, David. *Encyclopedia of Hurricanes, Typhoons and Cyclones*. New York: Checkmark Books, 2000.

Pinder, Eric. *Tying Down the Wind*. New York: Putnam, 2000.

Rosenfeld, Jeffrey. *Eye of the Storm*. New York: Plenum, 2003.

Sheets, Bob. *Hurricane Watch*. New York: Vintage Books, 2001.

Toomey, David. *Storm Chasers*. New York: Norton, 2002.

White, Robin. *Typhoon*. New York: Putman, 2003.

6 ······ Atlantis, the Mythical Land

MYTHS ABOUT ATLANTIS

Plato, the ancient Greek writer and philosopher, started it. In two of his books he described a glorious land of marble buildings crowned with gold and silver that had existed 9,500 years before his time (12,000 years before the present). What a glorious and exciting image! A fabled paradise filled with advanced and enlightened citizens, a land of ease and wealth—all now lost forever beneath the endless waves. But was there ever such a place, or is Atlantis just a fictional fancy of an early writer?

Plato described in detail mighty irrigation canals and construction that humankind would not duplicate until modern times, fruits and vegetation Plato (in his Mediterranean world) had never seen or heard of, hot and cold running water that would not reappear in human society until the twentieth century, and domesticated horses that would not reappear in the annals of human development for thousands of years. Most importantly, he described an advanced race of humans whose civilization, culture, science, technology, and accomplishments all arrived in the Atlantean culture at least 12,000 years earlier than modern science thinks possible.

And then the island nation sank beneath the waves. In a single day, Plato tells us, the entire Atlantis continent sank into the Atlantic depths and disappeared forever. What a day that must have been!

Through the 1700s the existence of ancient Atlantis was accepted as a given fact. But as science skills, research tools, and knowledge developed, doubts emerged. By the early 1900s, Atlantis had been reduced to a pleasant myth, a work of fiction by crafty old Plato. Everyone agreed that the final nail in Atlantis's coffin was hammered home by the emergence of plate tectonic theory in the late 1960s and early 1970s, America and Europe had drifted apart over the last several 100 million years. Before that they had fit together perfectly. There was no room for an island continent in the middle of the Atlantic. Atlantis was fiction. Period.

But more recent studies have found chinks in the armor of the Atlantis-is-fiction theory. Like a nine-lived cat, Atlantis refuses to die. New evidence hints at the possibility that a landmass *might* have existed in the mid-Atlantic as recently as 12,000 years ago and that advanced civilizations *could* have existed long before ancient Egypt (the first civilization from which we have written records).

Is Atlantis a myth, or could it be real? Could this prehistoric paradise really have been destroyed in a single fiery day of destruction? Suddenly the questions are back on the table for us to ponder, study, and dream about.

This myth of the destruction of Atlantis was compiled from Plato's descriptions combined with elements from similar myths from three other countries: the Portuguese myth of Atlantida, the Venezuelan myth of Atlan, and the Berber myth of Atlala. The descriptions of an island paradise with an advanced civilization are remarkably similar in each of these four mythic references. Each contributes its own details to the final day—the day Atlantis was lost forever. The reference to an Atlantan invasion of the Mediterranean and of a battle with Greek (Athenian) forces comes from Plato and other early Greek historians.

All versions of the myth agree that King Atlan was the last king of Atlantis and that he knew his island paradise was doomed before the catastrophic day on which it sank. The myth and parts of the science discussion that follow it were extracted from Kendall Haven's story on Atlantis in *That's Weird! Awesome Science Mysteries.* Presented here with permission of the author and publisher.

"The End of Atlantis," a Myth from Greece, Portugal, Morocco, and Venezuela

Early morning sun sparkled off the thin plates of gold that covered the dome of the great Temple of Poseidon, over 100 feet high and 600 feet long. Palaces and lesser temples of marble and silver radiated from it across the great inner circle of this capital city. Graceful bridges over perfectly carved circular canals joined buildings together, along with wide parks filled with breathtaking statuary. Towering sea-walls tamed the stormy Atlantic Ocean, named for Atlas, eldest son of the God Poseidon and the first king of these lands.

Towering above the sea walls rose the king's palace, built of black and red marble and lined with sheets of a red-bronze metal, called *orichalcum*, that shone more brightly than gold. Lush, rippling green fields spread west from the capital city for miles before curving up into the foothills of towering, snow-capped mountains.

The city and the land were more beautiful than a fairy tale.

But this spring day King Atlan was not pleased. A tall and muscled man, he planted himself at the seawall of his palace, wearing flowing silken robes sewn with gold threads, and he gazed steadily seaward. "What news from my brother's lands in the west?" King Atlan demanded.

A general, wearing a gold breastplate and plumed helmet, dropped to one knee and bowed. "Everything beyond the western mountains is flooded with sea water and has sunk below the waves, my lord."

The king slowly shook his head but did not turn away from the sea. "My scientists have been measuring shifts in those lands for over a month. Were all the people safely evacuated?"

The general nodded, "Yes, my king."

The same fate had already befallen two of the northern provinces. Over one quarter of Atlantis had already sunk.

The king had sent his great army east across the sea to secure new lands for his people to settle. For days the king had stood on this battlement, staring east, waiting for news of their conquest. "Have the engineers and scribes prepare our people for evacuation as soon as I receive word of the army's success," he ordered.

Two scribes began to wail and moan. "Our dear Atlantis cannot sink!" "What will happen to our great city? To my home and wealth?"

"Silence!" bellowed the king. He pointed toward the rising sun, shimmering like an orange disk just above the blue horizon. "Our future lies there before dear Atlantis sinks forever to the depths of Lord Poseidon's ocean realm."

The general protested, "Atlantis cannot sink, my king. It is the land given to us by the God Poseidon and by Atlas, themselves. They will protect it forever!"

"They have not protected my brother's western province," snapped King Atlan. Finally the king turned away from the sea and glared at a small, bent man covered in a ragged black robe. "What say you, soothsayer? Will the army's news be good or bad? Will Atlantis sink or reside above the waves forever? Speak, old man. I command you."

The soothsayer closed his eyes and hummed while his fingers seemed to paw and mold the air before him into a vision. "Where arrogance and cruelty reign, forces greater than Poseidon will gather to take revenge."

"What mean you?" demanded King Atlan. "It is not arrogance to *know* we are the greatest civilization on Earth. It is fact. All others are crude savages. And it is not cruel to kill those we encounter. They are better off dead than living in caves and huts as animals."

"Only Zeus is more powerful than Poseidon," muttered an advisor. "Is he saying Zeus will strike Atlantis?"

But the soothsayer continued without acknowledging the interruptions. "I see that the army's messenger will arrive this very day. But his news will do you no good, nor will you ever call him to your side to deliver it to you."

"Of course I'll call him to me!" The king waved his hand and sneered, "I asked for simple answers and you speak in riddles, old man . . ."

A slight tremor rumbled through Atlantis, causing the buildings to sway and small waves to ripple down the long canals. The king and his generals laughed. Small earthquakes were common in Atlantis. Most people ignored them as they went about their daily duties.

A second, stronger tremor rattled through the capital city, followed by a thunderous explosion. A boiling plume of ash and smoke rose from one of the lower mountains. Thin, red lines of lava oozed down its flanks. Screams and shouts of people in the vast city of splendor could be heard above the freight-train rumble of the volcano.

"My king, you must away!" squealed an advisor.

"Nonsense," scoffed King Atlan. "We have had volcanoes before in Atlantis." He snapped his fingers at his advisors. "When was the last volcano?"

A frazzled, gray-haired man nervously rummaged through scrolls. "Ah, here it is, my lord. Seventy-eight years ago, in the southern mountains."

"There," shrugged the king. "A common occurrence. Have my science advisors draw up any necessary plans to protect populated areas. And despite what my learned soothsayer claims . . ." The king paused and sneered at the bent, ragged man. ". . . It is the army's messenger I care *most* about, for he brings our future."

The entire top half of the volcanic mountain exploded in a ball of red-orange flame that rivaled the sun. The explosion's shock wave slammed into the glittering city, flattening people and trees. Water sloshed dangerously high in the canals that ringed the city walls. Towering fountains of glowing lava burst from a dozen gashes in the mountain's sides like a dazzling fireworks display. Building-sized boulders smashed into the city and raised great geysers when they smacked into the bay.

"We must get away!" whimpered the general, now trembling on hands and knees.

"Look!" cried King Atlan, pointing out to sea. "A sail! News arrives!"

"But the danger," whined his advisors.

The king snapped, "Have my engineers do what they must to protect the city and prepare the people to evacuate." Still pointing to the tiny white dot on the eastern horizon, he added, "I will remain here until that ship arrives. A king must look to the future."

The earth groaned and shook like a sapling being shaken by an angry bear. Statues tumbled. Graceful columns buckled and crashed to the ground in showers of splintered marble and dust. Walls cracked. Buildings screeched in protest and wobbled like rubber toys.

Tremor after tremor, rolling like one unending earthquake, turned the land to jelly. Buildings collapsed. Bridges disintegrated. A great cloud of marble dust and debris hung like a death shroud over the city. Great fissures and gashes tore through the land, creating instant canyons where flat city and fields had been moments before.

A second mountain exploded in a giant fireball. Jets of high-pressure lava sprayed 1,000 feet into the air. Fiery ash and molten rocks rained down thick as snow. A thousand fires roared through the city, spreading to join into a mighty funeral pyre for the great capital.

The screams of the crushed, burned, and dying were drowned by the thunder of volcanoes, the roar of the shifting earth, the whine of a gale-force wind created by the volcanic havoc, and the howl of dying buildings being torn apart.

Even as the walls crumbled around him, King Atlan stood transfixed, at the sea wall, straining to see a sign of his army's victory. "Look! The messenger stands in the bow eager to report!"

"We will all die!" wailed advisors and bodyguards, crouching to hide from falling debris.

Propelled by a strong eastern wind, the boat sped toward the royal dock. Now King Atlan could see his general's brother, the royal messenger, standing in the bow—battered, blood splattered, humbled, filled with bitter sadness, head lowered. The look said more than any detailed report could. It confirmed the king's worst nightmare fears. His army had lost. The Athenians had somehow defeated his unstoppable legions.

Finally the king perceived that deadly danger lay all around him.

Before the boat drew close enough to throw rope to dock, the water in the bay washed out to sea as if the ocean's plug had been pulled. The boat hit bottom and listed far to one side. Sailors were thrown across the deck like rag dolls. Bay bottom rocks, kelp, and clam beds were exposed to dry air. Canals drained to bottom mud as water rushed out to the empty bay.

King Atlan stood rooted in fascination. The ocean seemed to have disappeared. Slowly, his eyes were drawn far out to sea where the dark line of a monstrous wave began to rise, stretching across the horizon.

The land of Atlantis rose and fell like a twisting snake and rumbled like deafening thunder. Fire, ash, and billowing smoke hid the great city in a black haze. White-hot wildfires raced across the fields. Giant plumes of ash and rock rose from the volcanoes 60,000 feet into the mid-Atlantic sky. Rivers of lava raced toward the city and the sea.

The monster wave grew and built like a menacing shadow towering high above the city walls. Like a thundering avalanche, roaring in at 200 miles an hour, rising almost 200 feet in the air, uncountable tons of water slammed across the city, erasing every building, bridge, wall, tree, and sign of human habitation from the face of the land.

The land, itself, groaned under the onslaught of these millions of tons of water. The mighty wave boiled and churned all the way to the distant foothills. With a final trembling groan the entire plateau of Atlantis sank deep into the ocean, settling thousands of feet lower into the crust of the Earth.

Ocean water surged in to replace the land.

In a flash it was over. Waves, scattered debris, and muddy waters sloshed where fertile fields and palaces had stood. Circling gulls screeched in confusion at the loss of their perches.

All that remained of the mighty nation were a few scattered islands, the high mountain tops of old Atlantis that had not sunk, peopled by simple shepherds who had not ventured down from their mountain huts in years and knew nothing of the greatness of the cities, armies, and canals of the valleys far below.

Mighty Atlantis was gone.

THE SCIENCE OF ATLANTIS

The following beliefs are either directly stated or strongly implied in the presented myth. Here is what modern science knows about the aspects of the seas explained by each belief.

BELIEF: Atlantis existed.

Is it possible that a fabled island nation existed and then completely perished?

Before the 1950s, historical writings, legends, mariner diaries and logs, ship soundings, geology, geography, biology, linguistics, and archeology records were available for scientists to use to study Atlantis. After 1950 came scuba and sonar, which permitted humans to peer directly under the oceans. After 1970, satellites, computers, and the new plate tectonics theory were added to the tools scientists could use. In the mid-1970s, deep-sea submersibles were invented to actually cruise the ocean floor. In the 1980s satellite multispectrum ocean-bottom mapping was developed. Some of the evidence uncovered by these various scientific tools point toward the existence of Atlantis, some point against it.

There are four key points in the evidence against the existence of Atlantis. First, there is no direct supporting evidence to prove that Atlantis existed—no written records, no artifacts, no land, and no sites to study and catalog. Science cannot accept anything without physical evidence and proof.

Second, plate tectonic theory (currently accepted as fact) does not support the existence of a great landmass between North America and Europe. Third, satellite multiband scanning systems have allowed us to map the ocean floor. The mid-Atlantic shelf where Atlantis was supposed to have been is 5,000 to 8,000 feet deep. There is no evidence of any massive shift in the shape of the Earth's crust over the past 15,000 years. A large landmass couldn't have sunk more than 5,000 feet without leaving telltale traces and clues in the surrounding land and seabed.

Finally, modern anthropologists have developed a detailed theory of the timetable for the development of human civilization. The level of sophistication that Atlantis supposedly possessed comes 10,000 years too early to mesh with modern theory. (Cities weren't supposed to have developed until 4000 B.C. Man supposedly didn't domesticate animals until 5000 B.C. And so forth.)

So Atlantis is a myth, right? Consider the evidence on the other side.

There exists strong circumstantial evidence and some tantalizing bits of hard data to support Plato's Atlantis. In the late 1980s, an ancient African metal mine that is 43,000 years old was discovered. But that is long before a metal mine could have existed according to modern theory. Cromagnon cave drawings carbon dated to 22,000 to 25,000 years old at San Michele d'Arudy and Lamarche (both in France) show horses with bridles. But modern theory says horses were not tamed until 3000 B.C.

Giant stone ruins at Gozo on the island of Malta have been dated to 8000 B.C. and show advanced human engineering long before modern theory says it should have occurred. If modern theory can be wrong in these three places, it can be wrong in a fourth—Atlantis. The ancient Babylonian city of Nineveh was thought to be a myth until it was recently discovered. Maybe the myth of Atlantis is also real, its crumbled walls patiently waiting to be discovered.

The traditional lore of virtually every indigenous culture surrounding the Atlantic includes reference to a great island land that sank, destroying its advanced civilization. Every European story says that land lay to the west (in the Atlantic). Every story from a North or South American culture says it lay to the east (in the Atlantic). Most of these cultures had no contact with each other. Most of these stories pre-date Plato's writing. The story was written in stone by Egyptian and Aztec scholars, for example, more than 3,000 years before Plato's time.

Identical stories of a sinking Atlantic island grew independently in each culture. It is very unlikely that each of these cultures—separated by thousands of years and thousands of miles—could have invented the same fictional story. They had no direct contact with each other, and yet each claimed to have had contact from Atlantis.

Over thirty indigenous cultures surrounding the Atlantic have a name for this land that sounds like Atlantis—Atlala (Berber), Avalon (Welsh), Atlaintika (Basque), Atlantida (Portuguese), Atli (Viking), Arallin (Babylonian), Atda (Arab), Azatan (Aztec), Atlan (Venezuela), and so on. Only one, the Teutonic word Valhalla, is not remarkably similar to Atlantis.

An ancient Egyptian papyri now displayed in the Hermitage Museum in St. Petersburg, Russia, says that the pharaoh (in approximately 3000 B.C.) sent out an expedition to the west to search for the land from which, 3,500 years before, ancestors had sailed to Egypt. What else could that land be but Atlantis?

At least four other famous "mythical" cities have turned into fact in recent years when modern technology has made it possible to discover their sites. Homer's city of Troy has been discovered. The desert trading center of Nineveh (in Iraq) was detected by satellite wide-band imaging, as was the desert city of Ubar. The shuttle *Atlantis* took pictures that detected the site of the ancient Thai city of Ankor Wat. These were all dismissed as myths until modern technology found them and made them fact. Atlantis could be next on the list to be discovered.

Evidence has also been compiled on the ocean floor. In 1984, Dr. Maria Klenova of the Soviet Academy of Sciences reported that ocean-bottom rocks taken in samples from a 6,000-foot depth north of the Azores Islands (on the mid-Atlantic ridge) had to have been formed at atmospheric pressure less than 15,000 years ago. Dr. Pierre Termier, French oceanographer, studied ocean-bottom rocks about 500 miles south east of the Azores and discovered that they were a type of lava called tachylite, which is only formed in the presence of air and which will dissolve in seawater in 15,000 to 20,000 years. Both of these small studies show that what is now deep ocean floor in the mid-Atlantic (exactly where Atlantis was supposed to have been) had to have been dry land until around 12,000 to 15,000 years ago—just when Atlantis was supposed to have sunk.

Mid-Atlantic core samples drilled by the Unites States Geologic Survey (USGS) in 1980 lead to the same conclusion. They show a layer of volcanic ash laid down between 12,000 and 20,000 years ago—a sure indication of local, above-water volcanic activity. Finally, the mid-Atlantic plateau generally matches ancient descriptions of the shape and size of Atlantis.

Even more intriguing, a tip of ancient Atlantis might have been seen. On March 1, 1882, the British ship S.S. *Jesmond,* sailing from Sicily to New Orleans, found muddy water and millions of dead fish floating on the surface of the mid-Atlantic. On the horizon the crew saw smoke. By March 2, the *Jesmond* sailed close enough to see that the smoke billowed from an island—an island sitting where the charts showed no land for more than 1,000 miles in any direction.

The *Jesmond's* experienced British captain, Joseph Robson, led a landing party onto the barren, lava-rock island and, in two days of exploration, found arrow heads, bronze swords, and the crumbling remains of massive walls. He showed the few artifacts he took to reporters in New Orleans, who reported them in the local paper. The ship's log and all hands aboard swore that they had truthfully found a new island. Four other ships reported seeing mysterious smoke rising along the horizon in the mid-Atlantic during the same week. Their stories were reported in the *New York Times* and other east coast papers.

The *Jesmond's* British shipping company claimed ownership of Robson's artifacts. They were returned to London without further study and supposedly housed in the company's warehouse until they were destroyed by German rockets during World War II. Thus we will never know if they really were from Atlantis. Still, *something* happened out in the mid-Atlantic that March, even though Robson's island was never seen again. It apparently sank back below the waves.

There is a great body of circumstantial evidence that says Plato's Atlantis could have existed. However, no physical, tangible evidence exists to offer as proof.

The final question to ask is: *Where* do scientists think Atlantis sat? Various theories have placed it in the Sahara Desert, in Antarctica, in the

North Sea, off the coast of Greenland, in the Caribbean Sea, and in the Mediterranean Sea, as well as throughout the Atlantic.

Submerged roads and walls have been found by divers scattered across the western Caribbean—evidence of an advanced ancient civilization if not actually of Atlantis. Psychic Edgar Casey claimed that Atlantis would be found near the Caribbean Island of Bimini, but studies have discounted this area as a possible site for Atlantis.

In the 1970s Dr. James Mavor of the Woods Hole Oceanographic Institute in Massachusetts discovered that small Santorini Island (originally called Thera) near Crete in the Mediterranean had been blown apart by a massive volcanic explosion round 3500 B.C. This explosion was far bigger than Krakatoah, the most massive modern volcanic explosion, and blew out much of the island. A large chunk of the island sank during the explosion.

Several land sites on Santorini have been excavated and studied as well as areas that sank during the explosion. Evidence of a major port city of an advanced civilization was found both on land and under several hundred feet of water—a civilization that existed *before* the 3500 B.C. volcanic explosion. Both are currently being studied. With artifacts, photos, and hard evidence to prove that something was on Santorini Island 6,000 years ago, many scientists have accepted Santorini as the real Atlantis.

Maybe Plato wrote about Santorini and just changed the name, the location, and the date and exaggerated a few details. Maybe, but not likely.

The dates, size, and location of Santorini Island are all wrong. A small Mediterranean island nation does not fit with folklore and linguistic studies from all around the Atlantic—and especially from the west side of the Atlantic. Intriguing bits of pro-Atlantis data from the mid-Atlantic have been ignored and never studied to see if they lead to hard evidence.

But Santorini does establish that an advanced civilization existed at least 7,000 years ago and stretches modern theory. Maybe funding will be found to pursue the small clues that hint at Atlantis's existence in the Atlantic where Plato said it was. Without detailed (and expensive) searches of the mid-Atlantic ridge, Atlantis will remain an inspiring, but doubtful story.

BELIEF: It is not possible for whole lands to sink into the sea.

Certainly it is possible. The movement of tectonic plates eventually submerges lands that reach the edge of a plate. Wind and wave erosion eventually wear down an island and have sunk many low-lying Pacific islands over the eons. However, both of these known processes are exceedingly slow. They require millennia to pull a landmass under the waves.

But Atlantis did not sink slowly over hundreds of thousands of years. Is it possible for an island to disappear in a day? There are two islands that scientists have studied that were destroyed by catastrophic volcanic explosions: Santorini and Krakatoah. Certainly it is possible that other lands at other times were similarly destroyed.

A combined massive volcanic explosion and a tsunami (as described in the myth) are possible, but most unlikely. Any tsunami triggered by the volcanic explosion on Atlantis would have traveled outward—away from Atlantis, not toward it. The tsunami that struck Atlantis—as described in the myth—must have been generated by some other seismic event somewhere else in the eastern Atlantic. Moreover, that event had to conveniently occur at just the right time to have the tsunami it generated reach Atlantis at the same time that Atlantis suffered from its own earthquakes and volcanic explosion. Possible . . . but not likely.

BELIEF: Other islands besides Atlantis have existed and then disappeared.

Certainly a number of islands and cities have been reported only to then disappear under the ocean waves. Santorini and Krakatoah are two. The island sighted by the S.S. *Jesmond* is another. Mapmakers placed the Island of Saint Brendon in four different locations during the sixteenth century based on ship sitings. It was never seen after 1584.

Columbus lists Ursula Island in his charts of the Caribbean from one of his later voyages. However, the island was never seen again and only sparkling blue waters exist at the spot he claims to have set foot on it. The island of Hy-Brazil showed up just west of Ireland on cartographers' maps from 1325 to 1865 and has not been seen since. Buss Island in the North Atlantic was sighted and visited a dozen times from 1585 up into the early 1800s before it suddenly disappeared and had to be dropped from the charts.

Several Pacific atolls have sunk below the waves within the past 200 years. Divers have discovered submerged walls and apparent roadways at several sites in the Caribbean. That indicates that this land used to be above the waves and has sunk to a depth of eighty feet or so. More than forty other mysterious island sittings have been reported by passing ships—islands that were sited and then never seen again.

It is possible that the sailors making these claims—most of them experienced and skilled seamen—were either radically mistaken about their location (not likely) or lied for the sake of a good story. However, it is unlikely that an entire crew would go along with a wild lie. Someone would always blow the whistle and admit the lie—and no one ever has for any of these many sittings.

The only other possibility is that tectonic forces of the Earth pushed these islands above the sea only to later force them back to the ocean floor. It is certainly possible . . . but not proven.

BELIEF: We know all there is to know about the oceans.

The studies that have been used to debunk the Atlantis story seem to imply that we know all there is to know about the oceans. Nothing could be further from the truth. Modern science knows more about the surfaces of Mars, the Moon, Jupiter, and Saturn than about our own deep oceans. The best current estimates by leading oceanographers claim that 95% of the bottom-dwelling species have never been seen by humans. 99% of the ocean floor has never been seen or visited. Eighty percent of the ocean surface has never been visited or monitored (other than from satellites).

The almost 40,000 miles of mid-ocean ridges, the birthplace of new crust for our planet, have only been studied in a few specific spots, scattered thousands of miles apart. No giant squid—one of the most elusive and aggressive giant predators of the ocean—has been seen alive by humans for more than a century, even though scientists believe that thousands of them exist in the oceans.

It is most likely that the greatest wonders of the sea have not yet been discovered. They lie in wait, hidden deep beneath the churning waves, for the next generation of researchers to take up the call and descend into the mysterious watery depths.

— TOPICS FOR DISCUSSION AND PROJECTS

Here are activities, research topics, and discussion questions you can use to expand upon the key science concepts presented in this chapter.

Research and Discuss. Do you believe in the former existence of Atlantis? In other phantom islands? Do you think it is harder or easier now to believe in a "mythical" place like Atlantis than it was fifty years ago? One hundred years ago? Two hundred years ago? Why?

Research and Discuss. Compare the types of evidence used to support and to discount the existence of Atlantis. For example, which do you think holds more scientific weight: recent plate tectonics theory that says North America and Europe used to be joined, or linguistic and folklore studies that show that virtually every ancient civilization surrounding the Atlantic has a myth about a land whose name closely matched Atlantis? Which do you believe more? Why? Do you think Santorini Island is more believable as the site of Atlantis because it can be seen and studied (even though no ancient stories place it there), or the mid-Atlantic where so many stories say it was (even though there is no physical evidence)? Why?

Research and Discuss. Why do you think Atlantis (a lost paradise) has been so popular over the centuries? What makes it interesting to you? Do you think Atlantis would be as interesting if it had been inhabited by ignorant savages? Why? Can you find writings by others at the library or online who agree with you?

An Activity. Identify and research other lost worlds (for example Shangri-La, Babylon, Ankor Wat, lost cities of the desert such as Nineveh). Make a list of all the lost paradises you can find. Who believed/believes in them? What happened to them? Mark on a map where they were supposed to have been. Why weren't they ever found again? How did some stop being myths and stories and become historic fact? Mark on your map the lost cities that have been found again and note what technology was used to locate them. Were lost cities thought to be myths before they were found? What does that say for Atlantis?

An Activity. Create a lost world myth of your own. What will you call your lost world? Why? Where was it? Why? What special properties/attributes will you give to the land and its inhabitants? Who founded it—humans or gods? How and why was it lost? What would someone get if he or she were able to find your lost paradise again? Keep a log of the difficult parts and fun parts of creating your lost world myth. How can you make your story fascinating to other people?

SUGGESTED READING

Cohen, Daniel. *Mysterious Disappearances.* New York: Dodd, Meade, 1986.

Collin, Andrew. *Gateway to Atlantis.* New York: Carroll and Graf, 2000.

Donegan, Greg. *Atlantis and the Bermuda Triangle.* New York: Berkeley Books, 2000.

Ellis, Richard. *Imagining Atlantis.* New York: Alfred A. Knopf, 1998.

Haven, Kendall. *That's Weird! Awesome Science Mysteries.* Boulder, CO: Fulcrum, 1998.

Innes, Brian. *Where Was Atlantis?* Austin, TX: Raintree Steck-Vaughn Press, 1999.

Leonard, R. *Quest for Atlantis.* New York: Franklin Watts, 1999.

Nussbaum, Jay. *Blue Road to Atlantis.* New York: Warner Books, 2002.

Spence, Lewis. *The History of Atlantis.* New York: Gramercy Books, 1996.

Wallace, Holly. *The Mystery of Atlantis.* Chicago: Heinemann Library, 1999.

—— SUGGESTED READING FOR TEACHERS

Balit, Christina. *Atlantis: The Legend of a Lost City*. New York: Henry Holt, 2000.

Berlitz, Charles. *Atlantis, the Eighth Continent*. New York: G. P. Putnam's Sons, 1984.

————. *The Mystery of Atlantis*. New York: G. P. Putnam's Sons, 1972.

Bowman, John. *The Quest for Atlantis*. New York: Doubleday, 1991.

Cazeau, Charles. *Exploring the Unknown*. New York: Doubleday, 1980.

Donegan, Greg. *Atlantis and the Devil's Sea*. New York: Berkeley Books, 2001.

Flem-Ath, Rand. *The Atlantis Blueprint*. New York: Delacorte Press, 2001.

Freidrich, Walter. *Fire in the Sea: The Santorini Volcano*. New York: Cambridge University Press, 2000.

Johnson, Donald. *Phantom Islands of the Atlantic*. New York: Avon Books, 1996.

Luce, J. V. *Lost Atlantis: New Light on an Old Legend*. New York: McGraw-Hill, 1979.

Mavor, James. *Voyage to Atlantis*. New York: Scribner, 1983.

Thompson, Colin. *Looking for Atlantis*. New York: Alfred A. Knopf, 1993.

7 ·············· Sea Monsters

MYTHS ABOUT SEA MONSTERS

Virtually every ancient map of the seas shows evil, monstrous sea serpents lurking near its fringes. Every seafaring culture has a throve of stories that include giant sea creatures—some like snakes, some like giant dragons, some like slithering, tentacled squid, some like dinosaur-era oceanic reptiles, some described as looking like bigger cousins of the Loch Ness monster, a few even described as monster turtles.

Hoards of mariners up through the nineteenth century claimed to have seen giant and ferocious beasts in the sea and barely lived to tell the tale. Long lists of stout ships have been listed as lost to the vicious attacks of these creatures. Literally thousands of sightings and attacks by giant sea serpents have been well documented through the ages.

Ancient Greeks feared Scylla, a horrible monster that waited in the sea to smash ships. Aristotle, the world's first scientist/zoologist, described several species of sea serpents in great detail. Roman soldiers along the British coast described constant encounters with sea serpents.

Jason and his argonauts encountered several sea monsters and sirens during his famed quest for the Golden Fleece. Each was a minion of one of the Greek gods or demi-gods. Each was viscious and seemed intent on destroying all mere mortals who dared venture into its path. Sea monsters are evil and cruel. All myths and legends agree that it is so. But are they?

These monsters have been given fearful-sounding names such as Leviathan and kraken. Movies and fiction stories have often used monstrous sea serpents. In *20,000 Leagues Under the Sea*, the *Nautilus* submarine was attacked by a giant squid. *Moby Dick* is a book about a monstrous sperm whale with a chip on his shoulder. These stories resonate with audiences because we believe that they have a core of truth.

Anthropologists and psychologists say that humans create sea monsters because we need to put physical form to our unnamed fears and anxieties. Certainly the sea already possesses plenty of "monsters" for sailors to dread: cold, dark, and deadly waters, treacherous currents, razor-sharp coral reefs, and raging storms.

Some of the claimed sightings and attacks are easy to dismiss as fanciful exaggeration. Many, however, are not. The Glouster, Massachusetts, sea serpent was seen by more than 200 people during its ten-day stay near shore. Two British Navy ships and one U.S. Navy ship in the twentieth century have been attacked by monstrous sea serpents that were seen by more than 100 sailors in each instance. Two of these monsters appeared to be giant squid more than 100 feet long. One was described as looking more like a giant whale with a long neck and long front flippers.

Are there really giant creatures lurking in the sea lanes waiting to attack hapless ships? Are they really evil monsters intent on destroying human life? Are there mysterious, oversized creatures in the deep oceans that humans have never seen? Or are they merely sea stories invented to entertain bored sailors on long and idle voyages?

The myth that follows is not a classical myth. It does express the mythically based view of, and beliefs about, sea monsters. But it does not attempt to explain their origin. It is a modern story, only 125 years old.

Some claim that this account of the wreck of the *Carolyn* is pure mythic fantasy. Some say it is fact. I found the story of the sinking of the *Carolyn* in old naval records. There was a board of inquiry called, partly for insurance purposes, partly, I gathered, to determine if first mate Johnny Longden was murdered by the crew or not. The account presented here is based on the statements by the three survivors of the wreck. I have created specific dialog since they rarely included specific reference to what they actually said in the reports that I read. This myth and parts of the following science discussion were both extracted from Kendall Haven's story on sea monsters in *That's Weird! Awesome Science Mysteries*. Presented here with permission of the author and publisher.

"THE LOSS OF THE *CAROLYN*," A MYTH FROM AMERICA

The *Carolyn* was classed as a merchant ship sailing full out of Halifax, Nova Scotia, bound for Baltimore in August 1888. A trim schooner, she struggled through unusually calm seas for the north Atlantic with both masts rigged fore and aft trying to catch any puff of breeze that might wander by. She rode deep in the water, carrying 190 tons of cargo and a crew of eighteen.

As the sun set in a great orange ball leaving the cloudless sky to the stars, the ship's bell clanged eight times, the tones floating across an empty ocean. Eight bells was the universal signal for a crew change.

Johnny Longden, ship's mate, stood at the helm and ordered the oncoming watch to climb into the rigging and tighten the lines on each sail. His voice always sounded thin and whiny. But rat-faced Johnny Longden was as mean as a ferret and as tough as a wolverine.

"There's no wind to catch no matter how tight we trim the sails," grumbled Jefferson Kitlers, a short, powerful black man the crew called "Kit."

"You arguing with the mate?" snapped Longden.

"No, Mr. Longden." With a deep sigh, Kit scrambled into the rigging beside Samuel Withers, a red-headed Canadian who had been working flat boats on the St. Lawrence River until he signed on to the *Carolyn*.

Kit muttered, "I don't like a sea with no wind. Evil things rise to the surface of a flat sea at night."

"Evil things?" Sam asked.

Louder so all on deck could hear, Kit answered, "Aye. The Gods get bored on nights with a flat ocean and send out their children to attack mortals and provide some entertainment."

Someone on deck laughed.

Kit wagged a warning finger. "Don't you laugh and make the Gods angry. There's plenty monsters in the sea big enough to swallow this ship any time an angry God wants 'em to!"

Sam Withers grunted and nodded as he hauled on a rope for the fore top gallant sail. Maybe you believed in the Gods and sea monsters. Maybe you didn't. But everyone knew that many a good ship and crew had disappeared on calm nights just like this.

Ned Billings, one of the four crew just coming off watch, slid his harmonica out of a pocket and began to play to break the tension. Ned was only twenty-five but had been called "Old Ned" since he first joined the *Carolyn* four years ago. Everyone—except Johnny Longden—loved it when Ned settled into his harmonica. The music seemed to calm the seas. Longden hated anything that pulled the crew's mind away from sailing.

Jerimiah Coglin, the cook, and Billy Wolf, ship's cabin boy, wandered up onto deck, wiping their hands on aprons, to listen. Jerimiah was a lousy cook but always got the food served hot and on time. Billy was a thin, graceful boy of fourteen. Most on the crew believed he could carry a tray of brimming soup bowls in one hand across a pitching deck in a violent storm and not spill a drop.

Henry Wilton, ship's carpenter and the only white-haired member of the crew, leaned dreamily against the rail listening to Old Ned's notes drift across the water. His head snapped to the left. Something had caught the corner of his eye. There! A hump rising slightly out of the water a hundred yards off the port bow. He rubbed his old eyes, straining to see past the dusky twilight.

There it was again. A dark gray mound gliding through the calm waters. "Somethin's out there," he cried.

The music stopped. Most of the men dashed to the rail and squinted into the darkness following Henry's pointing finger.

"I don't see nothing."

"It *was* there, I tell, ya! A big hump . . . well, a *something*."

Jerimiah Coglin laughed, "Maybe the hump you saw, Henry, was a bloody *wave*." The sailors burst into a new round of laughter. "A wave in the ocean would be worth pointin' out, all right!"

"It's calm as a mill pond out there, I tell ya!" Henry snapped. "I saw something."

Old Ned blew life back into his harmonica and the crew forgot Henry's hump in the water.

As he slid back down the ropes to the deck, Kit eased over to Henry and said in a low voice, "I didn't see it, Henry, but I believe it. Nights such as this, with a hot, calm sea and not a breath of air, it drives the Gods crazy and turns 'em mean."

Several sailors gazed nervously over the rail, half expecting Poseidon himself to rise up and bellow his anger.

"Don't look for ordinary fish on a night like this," Kit continued. "With a hot, flat sea comes supernatural monsters that bullets and swords can't kill. That's what the Gods send out on nights like this."

Jerimiah Coglin nervously laughed. "You trying to put some voodoo magic on us, Kit? Pretty soon you'll spook the potatoes I got in the bin."

"I've *seen* them," Kit insisted. "Twice. Both like monster snakes over sixty feet long. Jaws big enough to swallow a man whole. I watched one pull down a long boat and I heard the screams of all six men as the monster ate them, one by one."

"I've seen 'em, too," said Samuel Withers, the Canadian, in a soft, solemn voice. "On the St. Lawrence. Something big and black glided up next to our ship. It was longer than I could see. Our whole ship pitched and rolled in its wake."

A rumbling vibration ran through the ship, sounding like the keel scraping over an uncharted mud shoal. Every sailor froze, bracing himself against deck and rail for another shock wave.

Captain James Blanchard stormed onto the deck wearing only the red long johns he slept in and carrying his cutlass. "What in blazes did you run us into, Mr. Longden?" Captain Blanchard was a giant bear of a man who could out-wrestle any two of his crew.

"We're in open sea eighty miles from shore," Mr. Longden protested. "There's nothing out here to hit."

"Well, *something* bumped against my ship," snarled the captain.

The *Carolyn* lifted slightly higher in the water and rolled ominously to starboard. Then the ship stopped dead in the water, as if a giant hand suddenly held it back. Timbers creaked. Spars and ropes groaned. The deck shuttered.

"So, the Sea Gods think they can play with my ship, eh?" Captain Blanchard roared. "Well, by thunder! No sea monster is taking my ship." He clanged the ship's bell. "All hands to deck! Prepare for battle!"

Henry muttered, "I *knew* I saw something."

Kit trembled. "I *knew* it was a bad night. The Gods need a sacrifice for their amusement and we're all going to die! I *knew* it."

Except for the gentle lapping of tiny waves, not a sound broke the eerie silence for several long minutes. Mr. Longden stood at the helm. Captain Blanchard stood nearby twisting his cutlass, chuckling like a prize fighter eager to enter the arena. The other sixteen in the crew were spread evenly around the ship staring into black, empty waters.

Hearts pounded. Mouths turned desert dry. Kit nervously kneaded the handle of a long gaffing spike. Old Ned tried to play his harmonica, but he found his mouth too dry to blow and his hands trembled too much to play a clear note. Even sailors who had been at sea for twenty years felt pangs of fear and suddenly longed for the safety of land so very far away.

Jerimiah Coglin swallowed hard to ease the throbbing lump in his throat and started for the hatch leading down to the kitchen.

"And where do you think you're goin', Cookie?" growled the captain.

Coglin's voice answered small and tight. "Thought everyone would be bloody hungry after the fight, Cap'n."

"Get back to the rail."

The *Carolyn's* bow dipped as if starting down a hill. The crew all wailed "Whooooooa!" and grabbed tight to whatever was near.

"I see arms, Cap'n," called young Billy Wolf, hanging over the bow rail. "They've grabbed the bow."

"Well, shoot the arms, by thunder!" roared the reply.

"Cap'n, I see a giant eye. Bigger'n my whole head!" called Henry. "It's lookin' at me."

"Well, shoot it, man!"

Henry raised his single-shot pistol. But before he could steady himself, aim and fire, a thick tentacle whipped over the rail and wrapped around Henry's waist. Thick as a mast and long as a coiled rope, the tentacle hoisted him high in the air as if he weighed no more than a feather.

Henry screamed and dropped his gun. The crew stared in frozen shock. "That monster's bigger than the whole bloody ship!"

Stout Samuel Withers dove at the wiggling appendage, sinking his knife deep into its flesh. The tentacle recoiled, snapping back across the rail. Samuel was thrown overboard. Still wrapped tight, Henry disappeared with a final scream into the black sea.

"Man overboard," cried the Captain. "Throw him a line."

Samuel didn't make it half way up the side of the ship before two thick tentacles locked onto his legs. As if he had no more strength than a child's doll, he was sucked under water faster than he could cry out for help.

Again all was calm and quiet on the sea. On board the *Carolyn*, all was terrified panic and pandemonium. Cries of "The Gods have abandoned us!" and "The monster will get us!" echoed across the deck.

"Silence!" bellowed the captain. "I will not have my crew disintegrate into a bunch of blubbering children! Man your stations. Fire or stab at anything that moves! You savvy?"

A long, terrifying minute of silence followed.

Faster than men could cry the alarm, three tentacles rose over the starboard rail. Two men fired shots into the water at the tentacles' base. One tentacle wrapped around a crewman's neck and snapped him into the water. One man hacked at a slithering tentacle with an ax until he was flung far out to sea. Jerimiah Coglin raced across the deck and finished the job, severing the tentacle with his long cleaver.

The monster withdrew. But two more in the crew were gone. Thirty feet of rubbery, severed tentacle flailed about on the deck. Ned reached out to touch it. In a final spasm, the thing snapped around his legs, locking him tight. It took three men to pry him free of the appendage.

"I think he's gone, Captain," cried Johnny Longden.

"He'll be gone when we kill him!" grumbled the captain. "The Sea Gods don't let go this easy on a calm, steamy night."

Five thick and deadly tentacles curled up to lock onto the ship's side and rail. The *Carolyn* rolled hard to port. Ropes, men, and supplies tumbled across the deck. Heavy cargo crates crashed across the hold, smashing into the wooden hull and springing several leaks.

Five men were flung into the sea as the grotesque monster tightened its grip on the *Carolyn*. One mast collapsed under the violent strain, crashing to the deck. Ropes and sheets fluttered down to trap the remaining crew.

Enraged, Captain Blanchard struggled to his feet and lurched across the deck toward the slimy tentacles, his cutlass in one hand, a long pike in the other. Jamming his sword clear through one tentacle to pin it to the rail, he snatched an ax from terrified Billy Wolf, who cowered in the main hatchway, and hacked off the limb.

The monster refused to release its prize and pulled harder, dipping the rail almost to the waterline.

"That does it, by thunder," yelled the captain. "You'll not get my ship!"

Razor-sharp pike in hand, the captain dove overboard into the heart of the frothing mass of tentacles to attack the beast. Sharks appeared and began to circle, hoping to feed on the scraps.

The rail dipped below the waterline. Ocean water rushed into open hatchways and sloshed into the cargo hold. Clinging to the broken mast stub, Ned could clearly see past the seething tentacles to a sharp and metal-hard beak that clicked and churned the water, eager to devour every living creature on the ship. He saw no sign of the captain, only his pike jammed into the side of the monster's gaping mouth.

The *Carolyn* was sinking. There was no longer any way to save her. Old Ned and Kit tore at the main hatch cover to loosen it from its hinges. Ned grabbed Billy Wolf by the collar and dove onto this makeshift raft as the deck sank below the rippling waves. Johnny Longden flung himself on just before the raft drifted clear of the wreck.

Coglin tried to splash his way to the raft but was cut short by a shark and disappeared beneath the surface.

The four remaining sailors huddled together, adrift in a sea of circling sharks, as ship, crewmates, and monster disappeared with a final swirling gurgle into the deep. Again the sea calmed, smooth as a mill pond, as if the *Carolyn* had never existed. The Gods had had their entertainment and fourteen sailors would never walk the shore again.

Three days later, two men and a cabin boy were plucked from the ocean by a passing ship. First mate Johnny Longden had mysteriously disappeared in the night. The three survivors all agreed on every detail of their frightful encounter with the Kraken—except on how Mr. Longden had disappeared. That remained, forever, an unsolved mystery. The insurance company laughed when the survivors claimed that the Gods sent a sea monster to destroy their ship and it refused to pay for the losses, claiming it must have been poor seamanship.

THE SCIENCE OF SEA MONSTERS

The following beliefs are either directly stated or strongly implied in the presented myth. Here is what modern science knows about the aspects of the seas explained by each belief.

BELIEF: Giant sea monsters exist (and are evil, intent on killing humans).

Science cannot study what it cannot see, measure, or directly detect. Sighting reports unaccompanied by hard evidence could contain subtle mistakes of size, color, or markings by an untrained observer that would lead to incorrect identification.

Scientists believe that most sighting reports are laced with a healthy dose of intentional or unintentional exaggeration and storytelling and are therefore unusable for serious study. To support this notion, they point out that reported sea monster behavior over the centuries has matched societal expectations and views on sea monsters rather than biological reality. In early sightings, sea monsters were all reported to be ferocious, violent, and aggressive. That is how people *expected* sea serpents to act. However, late nineteenth-century and twentieth-century sightings all report shy, harmless, and lonely looking beasts. Those descriptions match what human society *thought* about sea monsters during those time periods, not how real species act in the wild.

Most scientists dismiss the very notion of sea serpents and sea monsters as ridiculous folly, saying, "Show me some evidence, some proof, and then I'll study it."

It is certainly true that, as knowledge of ocean species has increased during the past century, reports of sea monster sightings have markedly decreased. It is therefore likely, say many scientists, that virtually *all* early sea serpent sightings—if they weren't the product of overactive imaginations—were encounters with ordinary ocean species we now know about.

However, the descriptions and size of the reported monsters are intriguing, and many sightings are too well documented to dismiss. Typical of the many reported and verified sightings are the following:

August 1817 and again in 1819, more than 200 Glouster Harbor, Massachusetts, citizens reported seeing a giant serpent-like creature, between fifty and eighty feet long, lolling in the harbor. Its head rose eight feet out of the water. It hung around for ten days before disappearing back out to sea. How could 200 people making multiple sightings over a ten-day period *all* be wrong? Yet there is no known species that fits the consistent description they gave of the monster.

November 30, 1861, the 100-foot French gunboat *Alecton* was attacked by a tentacled monster—presumably a giant squid. The crew decided to rope and capture it. However, it was so large that they could not secure it to the ship using all available ropes. The ship would have been dragged down and sunk if they hadn't cut it loose. That had to be one *big* squid!

March, 1896, a large blob of jelly-like tissue was found on the St. Augustine, Florida, beach. It weighed six tons and measured ninety-two feet from tentacle to tentacle. It was identified by Professor Verrill of Florida State University as being some species of octopus, "but far larger than any octopus on record." Other sightings have hinted that deep-sea octopuses might be as large as 200 feet across, but no species longer than thirty-five feet has ever been brought in whole.

November, 1958, eleven Brazilian fishermen fled from a sea serpent that threatened to capsize their boat. They each claimed the dinosaur-like monster was more than sixty-five feet long. The picture they each drew closely matched the Jurassic-aged plesiosaurus—the same species many think lives in Loch Ness, Scotland.

In June, 1956, three fishermen off Nova Scotia reported meeting a turtle whose shell measured forty-five feet across—more than four times the size of any turtle known to exist. The fishermen threw a rope and hook across the turtle to measure the size of its shell. The giant turtle kicked and dove, almost capsizing the fishermen's boat.

In October, 1971, Robert Le Serrec photographed what looked like a snake-shaped fifty-plus-foot-long sea monster just under the water near Hook Island in Australia. The photo has been studied and authenticated, but the creature does not match the shape of any known species.

April 25, 1977, while fishing off of New Zealand, the Japanese fishing trawler *Zuiyo Maru* hauled aboard a huge, decaying carcass more than twenty-two feet long and weighing three tons. It had a long neck, developed spine, fins, and flippers. Japanese scientists studied photos and tissue samples and concluded that "It looks like a *plesiosaur.*"

What are we to make of these reports: Wild stories? Intriguing facts? What does science make of them?

In 1968 Dr. Bernard Heuvelmans, eminent zoologist, published the results of his detailed study of more than 600 reported sea serpent sightings over a period of 150 years. Every legitimate sighting, he concluded, fit the description of one of nine different types of large, known sea creatures. Other researchers who have studied sea monsters generally agree with his findings.

Tops on this list are contacts with giant squid, the kraken, the most elusive and least known of all marine species. *Kraken* is a Swedish word for "uprooted tree," which is what a squid looks like with its ten tentacles snaking around like roots. A sixty-foot-long giant squid (the longest ever caught and studied) leaves sucker marks about four inches across from the tiny teeth and curved claws in the suckers on its two longest tentacles. However, sperm whales have been caught with the scars of squid sucker marks measuring over twenty inches across. The monster that made those marks would have to be more than 200 feet long, plenty big enough to account for even the most outlandish sighting reports.

Sharks are the second species most often identified as sea monsters. Large great white sharks can top twenty-eight feet in length and act every bit the terrifying monster. More often identified as sea monsters, however, are whale sharks and basking sharks (both harmless), which can grow to more than sixty feet. In 1972 a new species of shark—the megamouth—was discovered off the coast of Hawaii. This fifteen-foot-long shark find gave hope to sea serpent lovers around the globe. (If a fifteen-foot shark species can go undetected, then why not a plesiosaur or other prehistoric monster?)

Third are octopuses. Pacific octopuses can grow to more than thirty-five feet across, with 240 suckers on each arm. Larger juneville octopus have been found that hint that deep-sea monsters 200 feet across probably exist. Certainly an encounter with one of these would make anyone think of sea monsters, and such a giant would fit nicely with many sighting descriptions.

Fourth are whales, the Leviathan. Sperm whales historically have had a habit of beaching themselves. These sixty-five-foot-long giants are probably the origins of many sea monster myths and legends. Narwhals are native only to arctic waters and grow a long, straight tusk (a pointed horn that looks like a unicorn's horn) that stretches more than ten feet in length. Seeing this pointed spear rise up on a whale's head for the first time could conjure many a vision of sea serpents. Blue whales grow to more than 100 feet long and weigh as much as 200 tons: the biggest (heaviest) creature ever to live on Earth. (Seismosaurus and ultrasaurus were both a bit longer, but not as heavy.) Though not aggressive by nature, a frightened or wounded blue whale could easily smash a wooden ship and start a sea monster legend or two.

Other existing species match fewer sighting reports. Saltwater crocodiles (Southeast Asia) reach almost thirty feet in length and are exceptionally aggressive. Manta rays can also reach thirty feet across and, while floating on the surface, would appear to be big as a ship. Orafish (also called ribbon fish) are harmless snake-like fish that can grow to more than fifty feet in length. They swim with a vertical undulation that would create a series of humps on the water (frequently reported). Orafish also posses a red crest along their row of spiny fins. A red crest was noted in many sightings.

Viperfish and dragon fish supposedly live their entire lives in the murky depths of 1,500 feet to 4,500 feet below the surface. But they *could* rise to the surface and would certainly look like sea serpents. Both have long, undulating eel-like bodies that stretch more than fifty feet in length. Both have oversized mouths jammed with stiletto-like needle-sharp teeth. A close encounter with one of those would make any sailor believe in monsters.

Larval eels are usually very small. However, babies for one particular subspecies of larval eel have been caught that are six feet long. If their growth was proportionate to other larval eels, those babies would grow into sixty-foot to ninety-foot monsters looking very much like a sea serpent. Finally, giant seals can raise their heads four or five feet out of the water (a common description of a sighting).

These known oceanic species could account for almost all of the known sea monster sightings. It is still possible (but very unlikely) that some large prehistoric creatures or other unknown giant sea creatures have survived undetected. None, however, have ever been caught, captured, killed, or filmed.

Do sea serpents exist? Are there monstrous, prehistoric, dinosaur-era creatures lurking in the seas? It is impossible to prove that they do not exist. But in the absence of any concrete evidence to support the notion that such creatures still exist, the answer is as definite a no as an unproved answer can be.

Do sea monsters exist? Yes. The sea is full of giant creatures that would appear terrifying and monstrous to sailors in small wooden ships—creatures that adequately match virtually all reported sea serpent sightings over the past 200 years. The most probable candidates were listed above. However, current estimates suggest that humans have never seen 95% of all bottom-dwelling species in the ocean. There is plenty of room in the murky depths for all sorts of amazing creatures to roam.

···
BELIEF: Kracken attack ships and kill sailors.
···

Giant squid (kracken) are fascinating creatures. Shy and apparently sensitive to noise, they have only been sighted on a few occasions since the development of noisy combustion engines and propellers for ships. The pulsing noise has apparently driven them into the depths of the ocean.

The giant squid is a true mystery creature of the deep. Individual giant squid have been caught at sea measuring almost 100 feet in length, but they have never been brought back to land for study. Evidence exists of giants over twice that length measured from the tip of its arrow-shaped tail to its two, elongated arms that ripple like sea serpents far behind the squid's body. Giant squids grow longer than the length of five school busses, longer than the biggest dinosaur that ever walked the Earth.

Giant squids live solitary lives in the oceans depths. Life there is lived by sound, smell, and feel. Eyes are useless in the dark depths, though the giant squid possesses the largest eyes in the world, each eyeball larger than a basketball.

The squid doesn't swim. It soars, jet powered, through the water. A squid sucks water into its body cavity and then blasts it back out through two narrow side funnels called *siphons* at high speed. This exhaust water rockets a squid like exhaust gasses power a jet. Except the squid jets backwards, arrow-shaped tail first, torpedo body next, eighty-foot arms trailing behind. This jet-pack arrangement gives giant squids more speed, maneuverability, and raw grabbing power than any living creature in the oceans. No shark would stand a chance against this killer.

Teeth-ringed suckers on its two long arms allow the squid to lock onto any prey. Eight shorter tentacles—each as thick as a grown man's body—dangle in a circle around the two long arms, looking like wiggling snakes. The tentacles seem to paw the water as if waiting for a chance to wrap around some tender treat and pull it into the rock-hard, razor-sharp beak, as big across as a grown man's arm is long. Nothing else in the ocean can grab, twist, squeeze, crush, and hold as can the giant squid.

Yet scientists know very little about the biology and lives of giant squid. We don't know how many there are. We don't really know how big they can grow. We know very little about their life cycle—where they mate, where they give birth, how long they live, and so on. Our best guesses about basic life-cycle information for the giant squid comes from studying small, coastal squid. But no one really knows if the lives of deep-ocean giant squid are at all similar to what we learn by studying their one-pound coastal cousins.

Do giant squid attack ships? Yes, they have in the past. The descriptions of many sightings and attack reports exactly match that of a giant squid. It was surely a giant squid that took down the *Carolyn*.

· ·

BELIEF: Giant killer whales (like Moby Dick) exist.

Giant whales certainly exist. Blue whales are the largest creatures ever to exist on this planet. But are they killers? The only thing blue whales kill is krill, a tiny shrimp-like plankton. A single blue whale can eat tons of krill each day. Sperm whales are the biggest whale armed with teeth. Sperm whales eat fish and an occasional seal. There is no record of a sperm whale ever eating a person. Narwhales and killer whales (orca) are more aggressive and can threaten—or even attack—people who threaten them.

Actually, it is people who attack and eat whales. Populations of every whale species have plummeted, beginning in the early twentieth century when whaling ships became more efficient factory ships capable of killing and processing hundreds of whales each week. Several whale species are still on international watch lists and endangered species lists. Whaling of many species has been banned in most countries and curtailed in others.

Underwater sonar systems and sonar experiments by Navy ships and land bases also threaten whale survival. Intense sonar sound pulses damage whales' inner ears and equilibrium and cause severe inflammation and infection.

It is not whales that act as giant killers. It is humans who are destroying whales at alarming rates.

· ·

BELIEF: Sea monsters are all gone. They are things of the past.

Blue whales can grow to 100 feet long and weigh eighty tons. Whale sharks can stretch to sixty feet long. Gulper eels, viper fish, and sea dragons can grow to the same length and have spike-like, stiletto teeth several feet long in oversized mouths that look like movie nightmare versions of alien sea monsters. Best available evidence suggests that giant squids can grow to lengths of over 200 feet.

No, there are plenty of monsters (oversized creatures) left in the oceans—even if there aren't any that act like mythical sea monsters and attack ships. Scientists think that the populations of most of these giant fish are in decline. But some of them live in the dark depths and it is impossible to conduct accurate and complete population studies.

It is also probable that most of the species that live in the deepest levels of the ocean have never been seen. Who knows what creatures cruise the depths that have never been seen or discovered? Maybe prehistoric sea monsters *do* exist. It might be that wild images of fearsome sea monsters will turn out to be the truth.

BELIEF: Ancient sea monsters have been trapped in, and still live in, inland lakes.

Scotland's Loch Ness is not the only lake to claim a resident mysterious, sea serpent-like monster, but it is by far the most famous. "Champie" in Lake Champlian, New York, is the best-known American sea monster. There are twenty other lakes around the world that claim a resident sea monster. But no monster can hold a candle to the intrigue of "Nessie" of Loch Ness.

Nessie was first officially sited by Roman soldiers during their occupation of Britain around 200 A.D. However, local legend and story include mention of the Monster of the lake thousands of years before that time.

St. Colombo's biography mentions an encounter between the saint and a lake monster that roared and threatened to eat one of Colombo's men in 565 A.D. In 1715 the men who built the first, crude road along the lake's south side mentioned seeing creatures "big as whales" swimming in the lake. In the 1800s, sailors and workmen who built the canal system that connected Loch Ness to the Atlantic Ocean (on its south side) and to the North Sea (on its north side) also reported seeing huge monsters surface in the lake.

In 1933 a paved road was blasted into the steep hills skirting Loch Ness's northwest shore. Finally, it was convenient for people to travel right next to the lake. Nessie was spotted more than eighty times that year. By 1990, more than 4,000 sightings of the Lock Ness monster had been reported.

How could 4,000 people report seeing the monster without even one bringing back any proof of the encounter—a bone, a photo, a footprint, a scale . . . anything? If the monster were real, wouldn't at least *one* of all those people have been able to document an encounter convincingly? In the most studied, researched, observed, and photographed lake in the world, no one has ever produced one scrap of positive proof. That is enough to make anyone skeptical—except for the 4,000 people who have seen the monster and the several hundred who have seen tantalizing hints of it while conducting scientific research.

So, is the Loch Ness Monster a hoax or a real biological being? In a lake like Loch Ness, the question has proved harder to answer than one might think. Loch Ness stretches twenty-four miles long by more than one mile wide and reaches a maximum depth of more than 900 feet. Its average depth is more than 480 feet. Worse, the water has been turned a permanent yellow-brown by the thick tufts, scraps, and flakes of peat that have washed down from the surrounding mountains. Even near the surface on a clear day, visibility is less than forty feet. There is plenty of room in the deep, dark waters for a giant beast to glide like an unseen wraith past any detection effort.

What is to be made of these contradictory bodies of evidence? The least likely answer—that Nessie is the dinosaur-age plesiosaur, which roamed England over 60 million years ago—is the most popular with Nessie fans, partly because a plesiosaur's profile would match exactly the most commonly reported pattern of humps, neck, and head.

Some have proposed that Nessie is a giant turtle or a giant sea snake, but no evidence for such a species can be located. Others say the reported profiles match better with a small whale. Sea cows and basking sharks (which often reach more than fifty feet in length) could also explain many of the profiles reported by observers. Biologists point out that most of the reported "sea monster" skeletons that have washed up on small islands around Scotland have turned out to be the remains of giant basking sharks.

Many think that the most likely answer is that Nessie is a giant eel (several species can reach more than twelve feet in length) that periodically swims in from the sea. However, while it is possible for such a creature to swim the shallow river connecting Loch Ness to the sea through the middle of the town of Inverness, it would be highly unlikely for it to happen regularly without townsfolk spotting the creature coming or going.

Others point out that fish and eels move by wiggling their bodies side to side while mammals move their bodies up and down. Sighting reports more often mention that Nessie's body moves up and down through the water. Thus, some claim that Nessie has to be a mammal and that the humps are schools of porpoises, sea lions, or even giant otters that swim up the Ness river from the ocean. Without additional evidence, no one can offer more than an educated guess.

— TOPICS FOR DISCUSSION AND PROJECTS

Here are activities, research topics, and discussion questions you can use to expand upon the key science concepts presented in this chapter.

Research and Discuss. Do you think there are any sea monsters left? What makes something a sea monster? Do you think human activity affects giant ocean predators? How?

An Activity. Draw or build a composite model of what you think a "real" sea monster looks like. How big is it? What makes yours a sea monster?

Research and Discuss. Why do you think people have always wanted to—almost needed to—believe in sea serpents and sea monsters? Even people who have never been to sea or seen anything strange often insist that sea serpents are out there. Why? Is believing in sea monsters any different than children believing that monsters exist under their bed, or than believing in the bogyman, or in demons? What good do such beliefs do for humans who have them?

Research and Discuss. Usually, stories of encounters with sea monsters grow considerably bigger with each telling. The size of the monster increases. The danger to the seamen increases. The sailors and their ship seem to come closer to disaster with each telling. Why does this tend to happen? Does it happen to you with your stories? Is this bragging, or is this what naturally happens to stories?

An Activity. How big is big? Make to-scale model silhouettes of a 100-foot-long blue whale, an octopus that stretches 200 feet from tentacle tip to tentacle tip, a giant squid that extends 220 feet from the tail to the tips of its longest tentacles, a sixty-foot-long whale shark, a sixty-five-foot-long sperm whale, a twenty-eight-foot-long saltwater crocodile, and a human who stands six feet tall. Use the library and the Internet to find the body shapes and proportions for each of these species. What would you, the human, feel like if you met one of these monsters?

Research and Discuss. Collect stories of sea monsters and sea disasters. From which cultures and countries could you find them? Which stories seem believable? Why? Which sound like wild exaggeration? Why? Which do you think makes for a better story? Why?

An Activity. Giant squid and sperm whales are both now endangered populations, if not close to extinct. Make a chart of population estimates over the years for these two famous sea monsters. How numerous were they in 1850? In 1900? In 1920? 1940? And so on. Now prepare similar charts for three other whale species of your choice. Do you find a consistent pattern? Why have the populations of these species declined so dramatically? What factors or forces push these species toward extinction? What factors or forces are helping to save them?

Research and Discuss. Dr. Bernard Heuvelmans listed nine ocean species that account for most (he thought all) sea serpent and sea monster sightings. Pick one of those nine species and research that species through your library, through the Internet, or through oceanography departments of local universities. Here are some questions you can use to start your research. How long does this species live? How many are there? How many offspring are born at a time? Where do they live (territorial range)? What do they eat? What are their natural predators? What *don't* scientists know about this species? What are scientists still trying to find out? What makes studying these giant ocean dwellers so difficult?

Research and Discuss. Some evidence points toward the existence of a Loch Ness monster. Some points against it. How can a scientist decide what to believe? How would you compare the weight of 4,000 eyewitness accounts versus a single photo? Which do you think is a more reliable source? Which would you believe? Why?

Research and Discuss. Why do you think everyone has heard of the Loch Ness Monster but not about America's own Lake Champlain monster, Champie? Why haven't we heard about the monsters people have claimed to see in more than twenty other lakes world wide? In your opinion, what about Nessie has made her so famous and popular and kept the other lake monsters in relative obscurity?

Research and Discuss. Many scientists say that they are afraid to study Loch Ness for fear that they will lose credibility with their peers. Many say the same about studying sea monsters and sea serpents in general. What does that mean? What do they fear will happen? Are there other topics science should study but that scientists are afraid to tackle for fear of looking foolish to the rest of the scientific community? Do you think scientists have to be careful in picking what they will research in order to protect their reputations and their careers? Why?

An Activity. Conduct your own test of eyewitness reliability. Stage an "event" at school and then question other students who were eyewitnesses to see how accurately they remember what they saw. Any quick event will do. A good one is to have twelve students run across the school playground in a tight pack, in costume, screaming and yelling, and carrying signs. They must burst into view from a closed room, race at full speed making as much noise as possible, and disappear behind a building or into another room.

During the interval of from a minimum of an hour and a maximum of a couple of days, interview other students and ask them to describe in detail what they saw. Have them describe the number of runners, what they wore, their ages, what they were doing, and what they carried. Did different students remember seeing different events? How accurate are their descriptions? What does that imply for the accuracy of the reported Loch Ness monster sightings?

SUGGESTED READING

Angel, Heather. *Life in the Oceans: The Spectacular World of Whales, Giant Squid, Sharks and Other Unusual Sea Creatures.* New York: Bookthrift Co., 1996.

Bendick, Jeanne. *The Mystery of Loch Ness.* New York: McGraw-Hill, 1996.

Berke, Sally. *Monster at Loch Ness.* Milwaukee, WI: Raintree Books, 1997.

Bright, Michael. *There Are Giants in the Sea.* London: Robson Books, 1999.

Dipper, Frances. *Secrets of the Deep Revealed.* New York: DK Publishers, 2003.

Ellis, Richard. *The Search for the Giant Squid.* New York: Lyons Press, 1998.

Feldman, Gene. *In Search of Giant Squid.* Washington, DC: Smithsonian Press, 1999.

Garcia, Eulalia. *Giant Squid: Monsters of the Deep.* Milwaukee, WI: Gareth Stevens, 1997.

Garinger, Alan. *Water Monsters.* San Diego: Greenhaven Press, 1995.

Gleman, Rita. *Monsters of the Sea.* Boston: Little, Brown, 1996.

Haven, Kendall. *Close Encounters with Deadly Dangers.* Englewood, CO: Libraries Unlimited, 1998.

————. *That's Weird! Awesome Science Mysteries.* Boulder, CO: Fulcrum Publishers, 1998.

Heuvelmans, Bernard. *In the Wake of the Sea-Serpents.* New York: Hill and Wang, 1998.

Hoyt, Erich. *Creatures of the Deep.* Tonawanda, NY: Firefly Books, 2002.

Lanier, Kristina. "Legends of the Sea." *Christian Science Monitor* 90, 16 (1998): 43–56.

Lyons, Stephen, and Lisa Wolfinger. *The Beast of Loch Ness.* NOVA, WGHB-Boston, 1999.

Meredith, Dennis. *Search at Loch Ness*. New York: New York Times Book Co., 1999.

Osborne, Mary Pope. *Tales from the Odyssey: Book 3: Sirens and Sea Monsters*. New York: Hyperion for Children, 2003.

Perry, Janet. *Monsters of the Deep*. Milwaukee, WI: Gareth Stevens, 2001.

Pirotta, Saviour. *Monsters of the Deep*. New York: Thomson Learning, 1995.

Rabin, Staton. *Monster Myths: The Truth about Water Monsters*. New York: Franklin Watts, 1998.

Steele, Philip, and Martin Camm. *Sharks and Other Monsters of the Deep*. New York: DK Publishers, 1997.

Sweeney, Janes. *A Pictorial History of Sea Monsters*. New York: Crown Books, 1997.

Waters, John. *Giant Sea Creatures*. Chicago: Follett, 1995.

Zimmerman, Howard. *Beyond Dinosaurs*. New York: Atheneum, 2002.

—— SUGGESTED READING FOR TEACHERS

Abrahamson, David. "Elusive Behemoth: Giant Squid." *Rodale's Scuba Diving*. October 1995: 106–118.

Bakker, Robert. "Jurassic Sea Monsters." *Discover* 14, 9 (1999): 78–85.

Campbell, Steven. *The Loch Ness Monster: The Evidence.* New York: Prometheus Books, 1996.

Clark, Jerome. *Unexplained!* Canton, MI: Visible Ink Press, 2001.

Cousteau, Jaques. *Octopus and Squid: The Soft Intelligence.* Garden City, NY: Doubleday, 1983.

Drucker, Malka. *The Sea Monster's Secret.* San Diego: Harcourt Brace, 2002.

Ellis, Richard. *Monsters of the Sea.* New York: Alfred A. Knopf, 1998.

Jeans, Peter. *Seafaring Lore and Legend.* New York: McGraw-Hill, 2004.

McGowan, Christopher. *Dinosaurs, Spitfires and Sea Dragons.* Cambridge, MA: Harvard University Press, 1997.

8 ············ Mermaids and Mermen

MYTHS ABOUT MERFOLK

Few elements of marine lore go back further, are more persistent, or cause more problems for scholars and scientists than merfolk. Mermaids and mermen refuse to go away even though rational science has denounced their very existence for more than 300 years. How can people in dozens of separate ancient cultures have created the same half-human-half-fish mythic creatures that are always physically described in the same way when—according to science—no such creature ever existed? In nonscientific surveys of American viewers of the movie *Splash* (1992), almost a third believed that mermaids really do exist or once existed.

The early Babylonians worshiped a sea god, Oannes, with the head and upper body of a man and the lower body and tail of a fish. The children of Oannes became the first mermen and mermaids. The Syrians worshipped a mermaid moon goddess.

Greek and Roman mythologies abound with references to mermaids and mermen—some helpful to humans, some almost demonic. (With voices sweet but bewitching and deadly, the Sirens delighted in luring sailors to their deaths on the jagged rocks and then laughing while the hapless sailors struggled in the crashing surf and drowned.) Sirens tried to lure Jason and his argonauts to their doom. Jason was also tempted by water nymphs during his extended quest.

The word *mermaid* literally means *virgin of the sea*, like the goddess Aphrodite, who is often depicted being born of the foam of the sea and emerging from a giant clamshell with flowing golden hair—just like a mermaid. The mythology of the British Isles abounds with mythological references to merfolk, Blue Men, and other water nymphs.

So who are (or were) these mermaids and mermen?

Some say they were the descendents of the great sea gods—Ea-Enki, Oannes, Poseidon, Neptune, Njord, Kianda. Some say that merfolk are the remnants of minor river gods or that mermen and mermaids are created by the tragic drownings of humans. Some insist that it is just a case of mistaken zoology, the actual sightings of seals, sea lions, manatees, or walrus that the vivid imaginations of lonely sailors spun into mermaids.

All stories of merfolk agree that they are "near-mortals"—between gods and humans, between immortal and mortal. The stories say that they live in an undersea paradise and come to the surface occasionally—not because they need to, but because, presumably, they want to and like to. On rare occasion, merfolk come ashore in the guise of humans. Depending on the story, their motive is either curiosity about human life, a desire to help poor mortal humans, a desire to play cruel tricks on humans, or a need to take revenge for some wrong committed by a human.

Sightings of mermaids were common events in America and Europe through the 1880s. Sightings became sporadic over the next eighty years and have been virtually nonexistent since then. Did mermaids ever *really* exist? If so, what happened to them? The mythology of virtually every coastal people is saturated with reference to mermaids and mermen. But where is the physical evidence to back the stories up? None has ever been produced.

Mermaid stories tend to fall into two categories. Occasionally, merfolk emerge onto land, or allow themselves to be seen in order to tease, torment, and taunt gullible fishermen to their doom. More commonly, mermaid stories feature an honest, well-meaning mermaid who is wrongly trapped on land by humans. Sometimes the mermaid is released and the humans live on, sadder but wiser. Sometimes, however, thoughtless humans trap and imprison a mermaid and thus cause her death. Usually, this is the call for mermen to arrive, filled with bitter rage and god-like powers. Then woe be unto the humans!

This story, originally from Holland, is one such mythic story of arrogance, pride, indifference to the needs of others, and the revenge of a merman.

"The Merman's Revenge," a Myth from Holland

Long, long ago there stood a fishing port named Westerschouwen on the lovely island of Walcherer. Proud ships sailed out of that harbor traveling far and wide across the North Sea and bringing home rich cargoes. The people of the town grew prosperous, and then happy, and then haughty and proud.

There was no port to equal theirs. There were no ships as sleek and fast as theirs. They grew to feel that they were the rulers of the sea, and they bragged loudly—to anyone who would pause to listen—that their fishermen were the finest in the world.

One day six fishermen of Westerschouwen let down their nets into the cold, dark waters of the choppy North Sea and when they pulled them up, they drew back in astonishment.

"A mermaid!" they cried. "We caught a mermaid!"

In the net cowered a lovely creature. Her golden hair tumbled like spun gold, soft and wispy as silk, over her face and shoulders. Her slender arms lay helplessly intertwined in the rough rope of the net. Her slim, fishlike body was covered with green scales. Her graceful fish tail flopped and slapped against the dripping seaweed that lay in unruly humps at the bottom of the net.

The men of Westerschouwen laughed and pointed at their squirming catch. "We caught a *mermaid*!"

She begged them, "Please let me go. I will die if you take me away from the sea." Tears rolled like waves down her cheeks. "Please!"

"Let you *go*?!" jeered the men. "Do you think we're *fools*?"

Again they laughed and rubbed their hands eagerly together. "Every fisherman on the sea will have to admit that we're the best once we show them that we caught a mermaid," said one. "A prize like this will make us the most famous fishermen in the world," said a second.

"They'll give us a parade," added a third. "We'll be so famous, the mayor will declare a holiday!" All six fishermen cheered.

The poor mermaid wept in despair. "You must let me go. I beg you. I will die on land."

The fishermen roared their laughter. "We'll parade her through the whole town because they'll never *believe* we caught a mermaid until we *show* them."

The trembling mermaid said, "If you let me go back to my home and children, you will be blessed a thousand times over."

"What blessing could be better than a live mermaid to display in our town square?" jeered the men. And they crowded around and laughed and poked at her while she trembled and struggled and cried in the rough rope net that was beginning to scrape and chafe at her tender skin.

As they giddily hauled on the sails and turned the boat for Westerschouwen, they heard another voice role across the sea. It was a deep voice filled with thunder and sorrow. "Let my wife go."

"A merman!" cheered the fishermen. "Let's catch him too. What a prize *that* would be!"

"Let my wife go!" This time the voice slapped across the waves like a stinging command.

"Catch him!" cried the fishermen, working the sails and rudder to close in on the merman, bobbing chest-high out of the waves.

But they could not. The merman easily stayed just beyond their reach. When he rose in the waves, they saw that he carried a child, a tiny mermaid, in his arms. The merman's hair tumbled as green as the sea about his face and flowed over his foam-covered shoulders. His face was the color of driftwood.

The mermaid heard her husband and cried out to him and tore at the nets. But she could not break free.

The fishermen tired of chasing the merman. "What do we need *him* for?" asked one. "The mermaid is the real prize. She's all we need."

The others readily agreed. As their ship turned for Westerschouwen, the merman called, "We live in a home of shells and seaweed. My wife picked and blessed each shell. Without her, there can be no love in that house. She cannot survive on land and her baby needs her. I need her."

"Go away *fish man*," they sneered. "You can't hurt us and your wife will make us famous!"

When they reached port, they tied their ship fast to the pier moorings and hurried their treasure ashore. The townsfolk came running to see this strange, beautiful creature tangled in their net.

The mermaid wept and hid her face behind streaming golden hair as the townspeople peered and poked and snickered at her.

"Let's take her to the tower," said the mayor. "We'll lock her in the top room. Then she'll never escape and we can show her off to visitors and dignitaries."

And so the poor mermaid was imprisoned high in the town's tower.

The merman swam as close to shore as he dared. "Give her back to me," he called.

"Never!" answered the watchmen guarding the port.

"Give her back," the merman repeated, "and I will bless this town a thousand times over. But if you do not, then I will curse this town a thousand time *worse* than any evil you can imagine."

But the guards shook their spears and swords. "Be gone, *fish fool*. We are not afraid of you. Be gone, or we will send out our fishermen and they will snag you, too."

Every day the merman returned to the harbor and begged for his wife. And every day he was laughed at. And every day guards threw spears and fired arrows at him. He always brought his daughter and the tiny mermaid would cry out for her mother. But none of the townsfolk were moved by her plea.

A month and a day after she had been imprisoned, the mermaid died and the townsfolk were most annoyed that they no longer had their prize to look at and to make them famous.

As clouds boiled thick and low that afternoon, the merman cried out his curse to the seas and to the heavens. He swam his daughter back to their house of seashells and seaweed and he returned to Westerschouwen alone. He dived deep into the bay and brought up seaweed and sand. He filled up the channels where ships were wont to go. In a few hours every waterway was choked with sand and weeds.

The townsfolk heard his voice, rolling like the wailing wind, and they were afraid.

The wind began to moan, as if mourning the mermaid's death. Sand blew with it to peck at the townsfolk and torment their every step. Cattle in the fields mysteriously died. Haystacks and corncribs caught fire and were destroyed. Horses fell lame, stumbled, and broke their knees.

And still the wind howled and the sand blew. Like a tide that could not be stopped, the sand and weeds closed in on Westerschouwen. The hulls of fishing and cargo ships were tangled in weeds. Their decks were coated thick with sand. Some ships rolled over and sank. Many were locked forever in hills of sand—hills that grew to cover the masts and spars and crush the hulls.

Sand piled high in the streets. It blocked the doorways. It swept through even tightly closed windows. It turned each bite of food into sandy grit. It fell on the roofs until they collapsed. Sand filled the townsfolk's beds with a layer of grit rough as sandpaper. It trickled like itchy spiders down their backs and swarmed into their ears, eyes, and mouths.

And always they heard the merman's wailing voice calling from the harbor so that they wept with fear. The torment of the sand and the moaning wind drove the townsfolk mad so that they tore at their own hair and clawed at their own sand-scratched eyes.

Every tree, every house, every person in Westerschouwen was soon buried beneath the sand and dead—except for those six fisherman who were all trapped on their grounded fishing boat. There they huddled on the sand-covered deck and trembled and wailed with grief at the loss of their beautiful town.

The merman rose from the waves, fire glowing in his eyes. He stepped onto their ship and those fishermen begged for their lives. The merman answered, "Only if you will give me back the life of my wife." Then he killed them each with lighting bolts, one by one.

All that remained of Westerschouwen was the tower where his wife, the mermaid, had been imprisoned and where she died. The rest of the town—every building and every person—was buried deep beneath the shifting, moaning sands. Such was the revenge and the wrath of the merman.

THE SCIENCE OF MERFOLK

The following beliefs are either directly stated or strongly implied in the presented myth. Here is what modern science knows about the aspects of the seas explained by each belief.

BELIEF: Mermaids used to exist.

Early humans populated the land and assumed that there must be similar beings populating the sea and built their mythology accordingly. What we think of as mermaids trace back to the description of Atatgatis, wife of Oannes (Babylonian sea god)—long, flowing hair, graceful human arms, beautiful faces, alluring voices, no legs, fish tail.

Myths built around merfolk attempted to create an undersea culture that was similar to human life on land. Merfolk live in houses and sparkling palaces gathered into a garden paradise lying at the bottom of the sea. Merfolk breathe equally well under water or in the air.

Therein lie the two problems that science says make merfolk an impossibility. First, no light penetrates to the bottom of the ocean. There is no garden paradise there. If such a place existed in water shallow enough to receive significant sunlight (less then 250 feet of water), it would have to lie along some coast and would be easy to detect from the surface. Surely such a place would have been found since virtually every inch of the shallow-water continental shelves have been explored.

A bigger problem, however, is merfolk's amazing ability to breathe anywhere. Lungs and gills do the same thing—extract oxygen from the surrounding environment and pass it into the blood stream—but they are amazingly specialized organs. If we humans are left under water, we drown. That is, our lungs are incapable of extracting oxygen from water and we die from a lack of oxygen. We call it drowning.

If a fish is stranded on shore, it will also die. Its gills cannot extract oxygen from air and it dies from a lack of oxygen. The human and the fish would die for the same reason: the organ each possesses (lungs or gills) to extract oxygen from the environment can only work in one specific environment and will not function in any other.

Gills, however, are even more specialized than that. Place a trout in the ocean and it will die because its gills, developed to work in fresh water, cannot do their job in salt water. The trout dies from a lack of oxygen. Similarly, put a shark in your bathtub and it will die because its gills, designed to work in salt water, cannot extract oxygen from fresh water.

Young salmon undergo a transformation far more amazing than that of a cacooned caterpillar changing into a butterfly. Salmon are hatched in fresh water and, as they migrate through estuaries on their way to a life at sea, must rebuild their internal organs to adapt to salt water. It is a unique and truly amazing transformation.

There is no creature on this planet capable of breathing in salt water, fresh water, and air. There is no evidence that there ever was one. Yet merfolk would have to and science says that is impossible.

Finally, if there really were mermaids and mermen, then sometime, somewhere, someone would have caught one and been able to bring documented proof back to land. No one ever has. Scientists cannot study what they cannot see or detect. Without some proof, scientists say merfolk are a physical impossibility and the stuff of pure fiction.

On the other side sit countless sightings by seasoned seamen.

On his second voyage to the West Indies, Christopher Columbus reported seeing three mermaids "leaping a good distance out to sea" and found them "not so fair as they are painted."

On June 15, 1608, Henry Hudson and company (searching for the Northwest Passage) spotted a mermaid (flowing black hair, white skin, porpoise tail speckled like a mackerel) less than twenty yards off their bow. The ship's entire watch saw her, including the captain and all ship's officers. All agreed that she was a mermaid.

On September 8, 1809, William Munor, Scottish schoolmaster, reported seeing a naked woman sitting on dangerous rocks near the shore. After a minute she slipped easily into treacherous surf, splashed her tail, and disappeared underwater. Over next twenty years, four dozen credible, substantiated sightings of mermaids were reported in the British Isles.

In the summer of 1820, the crew of the *Leonidas*, sailing out of New York for England, sighted what the entire ship's company insisted was a mermaid less than half a ship's length off their port bow. The company got a good long look at the creature before she dipped back under the waves.

In 1855, a crew of four fishermen working out of the Isle of Mann (in the Irish Sea) caught a mermaid in their herring drift net, took her home, but could not get her to eat or drink. So they opened the door of the house where they held her. She glided across the beach on her tail and dove into the waters. Fifteen people reported seeing her before she was released. All described her the same way—a classic mermaid description.

In 1947, two old (early 80s) fishermen on the Island of Muck along the west coast of Scotland reported seeing a mermaid about twenty yards from shore sitting on a floating lobster box combing her hair. As soon as she noticed the two men, she plunged into the sea and was gone. Both men passed lie detector tests. They were convinced they had seen a mermaid.

More than 10,000 such sightings have been recorded by seamen and by those strolling along the coasts of the world. Shouldn't we accept and believe such an overwhelming body of first-hand accounts? But how can we when there exist no physical evidence and proof to back up the reports? Are all the people who claim to have seen mermaids and mermen liars? Are they all crazy?

Scientists say it is mostly a matter of observational methodology and observational objectivity. Scientists who have studied the mermaid phenomenon claim that what was actually seen was most likely a manatee, seal, sea lion, or walrus and that it looked like a mermaid because the observer (often subconsciously) *wanted* it to look like a mermaid and *wanted* it to be a mermaid.

What we want to see and what we expect to see strongly influence what we think we actually see. Police detectives are often given very different accounts of a crime by different witnesses, not because those witnesses are lying, but because what each one remembers seeing is strongly affected by what he or she expected to see. The same is true with sightings of mermaids, sea monsters, and aliens.

Scientists train to become objective observers. They have to practice for years to learn how to separate physical facts and observations from their own emotions and preconceived notions. As evidence, consider this: even though biologists have been going to sea for centuries, no trained biologist has ever reported seeing a mermaid. They have seen plenty of manatees, seals, and walruses, but they were always able to correctly identify the creature.

Does that prove that there are no mermaids? No. But it does make it highly improbable that they ever existed.

BELIEF: Merfolk have supernatural powers and mermaids use them to lure sailors to their death on jagged rocks.

In the story, an angry merman had the power to create mountains of sand and to direct the winds. Myths tell us that the Sirens of Greek and Roman mythology had the gift of irresistible singing voices and the nasty habit of using those voices to lure sailors into treacherous shoals that ripped the hulls out of their ships and cast the hapless sailors into maelstroms of foam, crashing waves, and jagged rocks. In Homer's famed account of the adventures of Jason and his Argonauts, Jason lashed himself to the mast so he could listen to the Sirens' call and not be able to respond to its lure. Jason made the rest of his crew stuff wax in their ears so they wouldn't be tempted.

But were one group of mermaids (the Sirens) really given such an irresistible, supernatural power? If not Sirens, what did the many sailors who claimed to have heard them really hear?

At times, waves of the correct size and speed, breaking on certain configurations of rocks and sand, will produce high-pitched sounds very much like a wail. If the period is just right, that sound can take on a rhythm that could be said to approach musical qualities. Combine that "enchanting" sound with sailors out at sea for a long period and away from the sound and beat of waves breaking along the shore, and they might think it sounded like music. Foam and spray from the crashing waves sets up a mist that dances and billows above the rocks. In the right kind of light, such a mist could allow a sailor's eyes to play tricks on themselves and on the sailor's mind. The mist might begin to appear like maidens dancing on the water and beckoning to the sailor.

That specific set of circumstances—which has been documented, observed, and recorded—is the best that science can offer to explain the reported sightings of Sirens. What scientists are saying is that it is possible for sailors to report seeing and hearing Sirens and be completely wrong in their interpretation of natural phenomena without actually lying.

Science can't prove that Sirens and mermaids (friendly and fiendish) don't exist. However, scientists can say with certainty that there is no proof or evidence of any kind that merfolk existed beyond fictional myth. Science can go no further in discussing merfolk and, so, can't discuss the motives and attitudes of these nonexistent beings.

However, just because no scientist has seen them, just because scientists have never been able to detect them in any way, doesn't mean merfolk can't or don't exist. Many sea creatures have been found to exist of which modern science was unaware. Many are mentioned in other chapters of this book. Many specimens have been caught at sea that could not be explained by current science theory and are therefore being ignored. Chapter 7 ("Sea Monsters") mentions several of these. Who knows what startling truths will be uncovered as we explore deeper into the mysterious realm of the deep oceans.

— TOPICS FOR DISCUSSION AND PROJECTS

Here are activities, research topics, and discussion questions you can use to expand upon the key science concepts presented in this chapter.

Research and Discuss. Do you believe merfolk exist? Have ever existed? What is the basis for your belief? What would it take to change your mind? Are there aspects of ocean science on which scientists have collectively changed their minds in the past century? Search for scientific beliefs about the ocean that were changed during the twentieth century. What did it take to change the prevailing beliefs of the scientific community?

An Activity. Here is an experiment that looks at the scientific method of observation. One person will prepare two trays of objects for the rest of the class to observe and then describe.

On the first tray, place ten small, common items, such as a key, a pencil, a watch, a paper clip, and so on. Uncover this tray so that the class can observe it for thirty seconds. Then cover the tray. Each class member must now describe the objects on that tray in writing. Give the class three minutes to write their descriptions before moving on to the second tray.

On the second tray (a large rectangular casserole dish covered in clear plastic works well for this), place ten bugs, spiders, roaches, earwigs, and so on. Uncover this tray for thirty seconds, then cover it again, and ask students to write their descriptions of these ten objects.

Now compare the two lists of descriptions. Which set of descriptions was more accurate, more complete, more objective, more detailed? Did your emotions and expectations distort your written descriptions of the second tray? Were you so fascinated watching the bugs that you forgot to consciously record the same level of objective fact and detail that you recorded for the first tray? Does this experiment give you any insights into why reports of something as exciting as a mermaid sighting might be inaccurate? Write those insights into an essay presenting your view about the existence of merfolk.

An Activity. Create your own merfolk and related myth to show their lives, origins, and values. What can they do? Where do they live? Why aren't they often seen? What do they want? What makes them angry? What powers do they have? When do they (and don't they) use those powers?

Research and Discuss. The biology of merfolk centers on their amazing ability to breathe in air and water. Research the difference between lungs and gills and between fresh water gills and saltwater gills. How do they each extract oxygen from their surroundings? Why can't they work in *any* environment?

An Activity. Mark on a world map the nations that have included merfolk in their mythology. By what other names besides mermaid and mermen are half-human-half-fish beings called? Keep track of the abilities of merfolk you find in the various myths you read.

SUGGESTED READING

Berman, Ruth. "Mermaids," in Malcolm Smith, ed. *Mythical and Fabulous Creatures.* New York: Greenwood Press, 1993.

Bertram, Georges. *In Search of Mermaids.* New York: T. Y. Crowell, 1997.

Climo, Shirley. *A Serenade of Mermaids.* New York: HarperTrophy, 1999.

———. *A Treasury of Mermaids.* New York: HarperCollins, 1997.

Coville, Bruce. *Half Human.* New York: Scholastic, 2001.

Dann, Patty. *Mermaids.* New York: Penguin Books, 1996.

Ellis, Richard. *Monsters of the Sea.* New York: Alfred A. Knopf, 1996.

Hoffman, Alice. *Aquamarine.* New York: Scholastic, 2001.

———. *Water Tales.* New York: Scholastic, 2003.

Manny-Sanders, Ruth. *A Book of Mermaids.* New York: Franklin Watts, 1994.

McKinly, Robin. *Water.* New York: Ace Trade Books, 2003.

Phillips, Ellen, ed. *The Enchanted World of Water Spirits.* New York: Time-Life Books, 1995.

—— SUGGESTED READING FOR TEACHERS

Clark, Jerome. *Unexplained*. Canton, MI: Visible Ink, 1999.

Eisenberg, Deborah. *All around Atlantis*. New York: Farrar, Straus and Giroux, 1997.

Jeabns, Peter. *Seafaring Lore and Legend*. New York: McGraw-Hill, 2004.

McHargue, Georges. *The Impossible People*. New York: Holt, Rinehart and Winston, 1995.

McKinley, Robin. *Water: Tales of Elemental Spirits*. New York: G. P. Putnam's Sons, 2002.

Ratisseau, Elizabeth. *Mermaids*. San Diego: Laughing Elephant Press, 1999.

Waugh, Sir Arthur. "The Folklore of Merfolk." *Folklore* 101 (June 1990): 73–84.

Wyman, Walter. *Mythical Creatures of the U.S.A. and Canada*. River Falls: University of Wisconsin Press, 1997.

9 .... Sharks: Kings of the Sea

MYTHS ABOUT SHARKS

Many people shudder when they think of sharks. Images from movies like *Jaws* flash through the mind—images of a mindless, brutal killer that attacks silently from the invisible depths of the ocean to maim and destroy. Even the word "shark" supports this image. It comes from the German word "*Schurke*," which means "villain."

Most people's image of a shark is both clear and frightening. Sharks are powerful. Sharks have cold, pitiless, black eyes. Sharks have rows of jagged, serrated teeth. Sharks seem savage, evil, and brutish. Sharks are carnivores, true eating machines, and eagerly feed on anything that ventures into their ocean environment.

But is that image accurate?

Sharks appear often in human folklore and mythology. They are god-like in the legends and stories from Hawaii and Polynesia. They appear often as pivotal characters in tales from ancient Greece and Babylon. Sharks are called the ocean's top predator, the kings of the sea.

But there are more than 300 species of sharks that inhabit the world's oceans. Fewer than a dozen of these species are dangerous to man. Only three or four come to mind when we think of "shark." But there is nothing in the ocean more dangerous than one of these few shark species while prowling for food.

This story, a traditional myth from the Hawaiian Island of Kaui, is typical in its treatment of sharks. Sharks are the villains, the evil ones who are also cleaver enough and powerful enough to fool and to outwit ordinary people. Sharks have god-like powers and can only be defeated through the use of other gods or the magic sorcery of a *kahuna*.

"How Sharks Came to Live in the Sea," a Myth from the Island of Kaui, Hawaii

Early each morning when the sun still rested on *Wai'ale'ale* (the ocean waves) and before it leapt into the sky, the fishermen of Mana arose from their beds. They walked the narrow trail from the village past the cultivated fields of Kawelo, the farmer, and so to their fishing canoes beached next to the sea.

No matter how early they left, Kawelo was already in his *uala* (sweet potato) fields. His *kihei* (Hawaiian shawl) was always knotted at his right shoulder, covering him from neck to heel from the cool morning air.

Kawelo always clutched the edge of his *kihei* as the morning breezes tugged at it and waved with his other hand at the passing fishermen. "It is a good day, men of Mana!" he would call. "Be sure the bananas are put away!"

The men would nod and smile appreciatively. For all knew that it brought bad luck for anyone to directly mention fishing to a fisherman on his way to fish or for any woman to eat a banana while her husband was out fishing. "What a pleasant and proper fellow Kawelo is," they would say as they waved and walked on.

"And he grows the sweetest potatoes," added another of the men.

"Be careful near the sea," Kawelo would call as they passed. "The shark has not had his breakfast yet and you might be swallowed head and tail!"

As the sun grew higher, the women of Mana walked along the path that passed Kawelo's farm on their way to the marshes to pick reeds to weave into *luau* mats.

Kawelo clutched his *kihei* and waved as he squatted, working in his *uala* field. "Good morning women. It is a beautiful day for weaving."

The women nodded and continued along the path saying, "He is very pleasantly spoken." And, "He always has a cheerful word to say." And "He is very hard working. That's why he grows the best sweet potatoes."

As they passed, Kawelo called to them, "Be careful at the beach. The shark has not yet had his breakfst."

Soon, the children of Mana passed by on their way to the beach to swim. "It is a beautiful day for swimming," Kawelo called. "But take care. The shark could swallow you head and tail and he has not yet had his breakfast."

The children laughed and answered, "We will be careful." And "We will not become the shark's breakfast." To each other they added, "He is a nice man, but he works too hard and he worries to much about the shark."

Soon after the children had gone, Kawelo stood up. "Aye," he said, "the shark has not yet had his breakfast."

Kawelo walked to the shore and slipped along a hidden path through the dunes. He saw with satisfaction that the fishermen were far out to sea in their canoes, that the women were absorbed with their weaving along the shore where the marshes emptied into the sea, and that the children were frolicking in the surf. All had forgotten his warning.

Kawelo untied his *kihei*, laying bare the secret the morning breezes had tried to show the people of Mana. The great shark's mouth on his back smiled as Kawelo slipped into the water and changed back into a fearsome shark gliding with ease through the shifting curtains of light that shimmered through the silent waters of the lagoon. A shark god, Kawelo could change into 400 forms. But he was, above all, a shark—a hungry shark who had not yet had his breakfast.

Kawelo gazed up through the pale green water to where the children played in the surf. He watched one especially daring boy swim far out from shore. Like a surging bolt of lightning, Kawelo shot up through his watery home and caught the boy in his razor teeth and mighty jaws. The monster rose half out of the water and laughed as he tossed the boy's body into the air and watched frozen fear race across the faces of the other children and women. And just that fast, the boy was gone and the shark swam into the depths, contented with his delicious breakfast.

Day after day, it was the same. The shark always managed to find a victim—sometimes a fisherman who dove from his canoe to gather shellfish; sometimes a woman who cooled herself in the ocean at midday or stepped into the sea to soak the reeds she would weave in the afternoon; sometimes a child who grew too bold in his or her play.

Sometimes the people of Mana would grow afraid and stay away from the sea. Then Kawelo would work in his fields and wave pleasant greetings to all who passed. The shark god might be hungry, but he was also patient. Soon enough, the people of Mana would forget their fears and remember the joy of the sea. The sea would again call to them and Kawelo would have his breakfast once more.

Then one day, as the people of Mana grieved over the loss of the chief's daughter to the jaws of the shark, they turned angry.

"How long must these killings go on?" demanded one woman. "Why doesn't anyone *do* something?" The reproach in her voice stung the men of Mana.

"We will kill the shark!" they cried and rushed to the shore with spears and clubs and paddled out into the ocean to search for the shark.

There was no one left in Mana to hear Kawelo laugh as he worked in his *uala* field. "Fools!" he jeered, "You will never catch me for I am far too clever to be caught by simple fools."

After many days, the people of Mana gave up searching for the shark. Walking to and from the sea they always passed Kawelo, who clutched his *kihei* and greeted them from his fields.

"Poor Kawelo," they said. "Such a nice man, but he works too hard. See? He is becoming skinny and underfed because he works so hard."

Soon the people decided that the shark had gone and went back to their old ways, and again the shark had his breakfast and was full and happy.

Now the people believed that the gods had sent the shark as a plague to torment them. They gathered a great feast of pig, mango, chicken, papaya, and fish and carried these to the *heiau* (temple) at Polihale and laid the feast at the feet of the *kahuna kiloilo* (head priest and sorcerer).

"Help us!" they begged. "Rid us of the monster who eats us."

The *kahuna* poured water from the lagoon at Mana's beach into a calabash and dropped in a *kilo pohaku* (seeing stone) that gave reflections of the truth locked in the water.

The *kahuna* gazed into the calabash. First he saw a giant shark laughing and opening his mighty jaws. The *kahuna* nodded. "This is not an ordinary shark. It is a *kapuna* (a demon of supernatural powers)."

The villagers of Mana gasped and shuttered and moaned.

The *kahuna* called for silence and continued to watch the seeing stone. Next he saw a tapa *kihei* flapping in the wind trying to lift itself. Then he saw an image of a small fish, then of a sweet potato vine. Then the calabash filled with an image of the night sky with one star standing forth, shining brighter than any other.

Then again he saw the shark. But the shark's image changed from shark to worm, to butterfly, to caterpillar, to rat, to man, and back to shark. Faster and faster so that the images became a blur.

Then the images faded and the *kahuna* nodded in understanding. A demon shark god who could assume any form and had come down from the stars to live among the people of Mana and eat them. "The shark you seek does not live in the sea," he said. "He lives among you surrounded by *uala* vines."

"Kawelo?!" the people gasped. But he was always so pleasant. He works so hard in his *uala* field. How could he be the demon who was eating them?

Then they thought of all the village men, women, and children the shark had eaten and they cried, "Kill him!"

"Wait!" called the *kahuna*. "He is a *kapuna* and not easy to kill. You must weave two nets—one strong enough to hold the shark, and one with a mesh so fine it will snare the feet of a butterfly. Drag the monster onto shore. Pitch him into a deep *imu* [in-ground cooking pit]. Keep the fire burning bright red and hot as lava for five times ten days and finally cover every ash with dry dirt. Then the shark will trouble you no more."

The people of Mana wove the two nets and stretched the big one across the cove, secured to two mighty trees. Then the men pretended to fish just outside the line of the net and the children pretended to play in the surf.

"What fools!" thought Kawelo. "They play and fish with no thought to their coming deaths. It is time for the shark to have his breakfast."

Swiftly he threw aside his *kihei* and dove into the protected waters of the lagoon. He cruised along the bottom, watching the people, picking his target for the day. There, a plump boy swimming just outside the surf line. It was time for the shark to eat and show his superiority to the people of Mana.

Now at full speed, the shark raced up and forward—and smashed into the net. The fishermen yelled and struck the water with their paddles. The women and children pulled on the net's ropes to tighten the circle.

The shark was confused by the net and by the noise. But he quickly recovered and fought against the net with all his mighty strength. He tore at it with his razor teeth. But the thick fibers, woven as the *kuhana* had directed, would not break. He lashed out with his tail, knocking men from their canoes with each swing.

But the net held and the men quickly rose to continue their pulling. The massive shark was slowly dragged toward shore. Kawelo changed into a small fish and tried to swim under the net. But the *kahuna* had told the people to weight the bottom so that it would scrape along the ocean's floor. The little fish could not escape under the net.

Kawelo changed himself into a sea slug and sank into the sandy bottom, hoping the net would slide over him, but it did not.

Kawelo grew enraged and changed back into a shark, lunging at first one fisherman and then at another, hoping they would be frightened and drop the net. But they thought of their lost children and they held tight.

As he was dragged onto the sandy beach, the shark turned back into pleasant Kawelo. "Do not hurt me. I am Kawelo, your neighbor. I am the one who grows the sweet potatoes for you to eat."

But the men laughed. "I see the shark's mouth on your back. You are the shark who eats us and you must die!"

Kawelo turned himself into a butterfly and tried to fly through the holes in the great net. But the women spread the second net and tossed it over him. The butterfly was snared in the fine mesh and sank to the sand.

Gasping for breath, Kawelo turned himself back into the shark that he was, vicious, deadly, and dangerous. His tail lashed. His mighty jaws snapped. But the people thought of all the villagers he had eaten and were brave. They tossed Kawelo into a deep *imu* that was filled with stones heated red hot. Then they tossed in more wood and kept the fire burning bright red and lava hot for ten times five days.

Then the people rejoiced, thinking that the shark was finally dead. They ran to the beach to celebrate their freedom, leaving the *imu* uncovered with dry dirt.

But a *kupuna* shark is not an easy thing to kill for it holds power beyond ordinary people's imagining. Though he was burned to ashes, Kawelo used his last strength to summon a rain—a drenching rain. The rain swelled the streams and marsh to over-flowing. The rain water crept into the *imu* and lifted Kawelo's ashes up to flow with the flood waters down to the sea.

As each gray ash touched salt water, it turned into a small gray shark—a shark that was hungry for its breakfast.

In the morning the people of Mana looked out over the lagoon. They were dismayed to see thousands of shark fins gliding through the water. The ocean was even more dangerous than before.

"Fools!" scolded the *kahuna*. "You did not do everything I told you to."

From then on, whenever the people of Mana passed by Kawelo's old farm on their way to the sea, they sadly remembered his daily warning, "Be careful. The shark has not yet had his breakfast."

And the people of Mana knew that now thousands of hungry sharks circled their island and that none of them had had enough breakfast.

And that is how there came to be so many sharks in the ocean today.

THE SCIENCE OF SHARKS

The following beliefs are either directly stated or strongly implied in the presented myth. Here is what modern science knows about the aspects of the seas explained by each belief.

BELIEF: Sharks are all killers—man-eaters.

Fish, like land animals, may be divided into two general groups: plant eaters and meat eaters. Plant-eating fish eat plankton (floating microscopic plants with names like diatoms and dinoflagelates) augmented with nibbles of seaweed and sea grasses. There are also tiny planktonic animals (zooplankton like krill) that are munched by grazing fish from tiny reef fish up to sixty-foot-long basking sharks and giant blue whales.

All other fish eat other fish. Most sharks are carnivores and eat fish. Small sharks eat tiny bay and reef fish. Large sharks (tiger, bull, hammerhead, leopard, great white) eat larger fish and (their favorite meal) seals and sea lions. Some sharks (basking shark and whale shark) are plant eaters. Only the biggest four or five species of the carnivore sharks are capable of attacking and severely damaging a human.

By current estimates, there are over a billion sharks in the world divided among more than 300 shark varieties—from tiny bay sharks only six inches long to giant whale sharks that stretch over sixty feet long. Some sharks are shy and nonaggressive by nature—even timid (like the nurse shark). Some are aggressive and territorial (such as the tiger shark).

Most sharks, like other fish, are cold blooded. Eight shark species, however, (including great whites) are warm blooded and have to gobble enormous amounts of food to produce the necessary heat to maintain their body temperature. We don't know why they don't freeze. We would. But without the great layers of fat and blubber that whales, seals, walruses, and sea lions rely on for insulation, these shark species maintain a body temperature close to that of humans while living in the chill ocean waters that would quickly kill a human. Scientists do not know how they do it.

Sharks come in every size, configuration, and personality. Sharks live in all seas and bays. Sharks are everywhere outside the polar regions and have successfully survived in the seas since before the earliest dinosaur set foot on land.

Only four or five shark species are capable of attacking a person and none really want to. Even tiger sharks, the most dangerous and aggressive, and great whites, the species responsible for the most human attacks, are in far greater danger from humans than humans are from them. The vast majority of shark species have never, and will never, threaten or attack any human swimmer in the ocean.

FIGURE 9.1 • Profiles of Major Shark Species

Basking Shark

Great White
Shark

Bull Shark

Tiger Shark

Leopard Shark

Hammerhead Shark

Viewing the variety that is possible within the family of sharks brings a question to mind. What makes a shark a shark? What *is* a shark?

All sharks lack three things that make them unique among fishes. First, sharks are the only fish without a swim bladder (an adjustable gas-filled bladder that keeps fish in perfect balance with the water, neither tending to float up nor sink down unless they want to). All sharks would slowly sink if they stopped their endless swim. A number of Caribbean sharks have been seen resting on the ocean floor, seemingly asleep. They sank to the sandy bottom because they stopped swimming.

Second, sharks lack the ability to pump water across their gills. Gills do for a fish what your lungs do for you. Gills draw oxygen out of the water and pass it into the fish's bloodstream. Most fish have sets of mussels that pump water in through their mouths and out across their gills. Sharks do not. They must either forever move or face into a moving current in order to breathe.

Third, sharks have no bones—no bones at all. Their skeletons are made entirely of cartilage (like the bridge of your nose). Cartilage, like skin and muscle, disintegrate after death. When a shark dies, all that is left is a pile of deadly, serrated teeth. However, having no bones makes sharks uniquely flexible and maneuverable—something that has helped their incredible success over the eons.

Five additional factors have contributed to sharks' amazing survival record.

1. Sharks are one of the few ocean species not deposited as eggs by the mother to develop on their own. Sharks are born alive and are instantly capable of swimming, hunting, and eating, their first full set of teeth ready and in position at birth.

2. Sharks hunt both day and night, unlike almost every other major predator species on Earth.

3. Sharks are born with an almost inexhaustible supply of teeth. When one breaks off, a replacement tooth lies tucked against the gums, like the next page of a book, awaiting its turn to flip into position in the jaw. Interestingly, each new tooth is slightly larger than the one it replaces. Over the years, a shark's teeth grow bigger and more lethal.

4. The shark does not feel pain. It has no nervous system to detect and measure pain. No matter what happens to a shark, it keeps on going.

5. Finally, a shark will eat anything, so that as the food web around it changes, a shark's ability to hunt and eat is not affected.

Sharks are unique. They are evolutionary successes. They are tireless and skilled hunters. But—with the exception of tiger, bull, leopard, and great white sharks—they are not "man-eaters." Even those three species do not seek out humans for their feasts.

··

BELIEF: Sharks are kings of the ocean.

Sharks are top predators in their ecosystem—as are lions, tigers, grizzly bears, anaconda, komodo dragons, and other major predators on land. But not all sharks occupy this ecological niche. When thinking of sharks as top predators, we are really referring to five specific shark species: great white, tiger, leopard, bull, and hammerhead sharks.

As some of the ocean's top predators, these shark species may be called "kings of the ocean." They deserve the title every bit as much as the lion does. But they are not alone at the top of the oceanic food web. Killer whales, sperm whales, and giant squid can also make a claim on the title. If sharks hold an undisputed claim to the top, it is as top predator in shallow coastal waters and along the world's coral reefs.

The other distinction sharks can claim is longevity. Sharks have existed, virtually unchanged, for 650 million years. No other ocean predator can claim that kind of endurance.

Yet for all of this fame and survivability, scientists know amazingly little about these tops shark species. Great whites are known to cluster in three specific spots: Dangerous Reef in Australia, Dyer Island off South Africa, and the California coast between the Farallon Islands (chunks of rock thrust above the water ten miles outside San Francisco Bay) and the Sonoma County coast fifty miles to the north.

However, no data at all has been collected on great whites across 95% of their natural range. Their population is plummeting worldwide—primarily because of humans. This creature has survived for 650 million years, but if we are not careful, humans will wipe them out within fifty years. Scientists know almost nothing about their population dynamics or reproductive behavior. Great whites are the most efficient, high-tech hunters on Earth and human action might wipe them out before we learn how they do the amazing things they can do. Even more frightening, scientists know far more about great whites than they do about any other shark species.

Sharks may be "kings of the ocean," but without help and protection, their reign may soon be over.

....

BELIEF: Sharks can smell victims miles away.

This belief is true. Sharks possess the most incredible sensory system in the world. Sharks are swimming computers that can sense light, sound, electrical fields, magnetic fields, and vibrations. They sense every creature within a half mile.

A shark's long-range sense of smell is as sensitive and accurate as that of any species on Earth. Two-thirds of a shark's brain is devoted to the sense of smell.

But smell isn't their only long-range detection system. Like a second, long-distance set of ears, most shark species have liquid-filled tubes, called *lateral lines*, running the length of their bodies. These lines detect low-frequency vibrations from miles away. The regular beating of a fish's tail or the splashing of a swimmer could be detected by these lateral lines from almost a mile away.

At a range of fifty to eighty yards, the shark abandons its long-range sensors and relies on sight and hearing to identify a target. But even more than sight, the shark hones in on its prey using *electro-receptors*, small glands located near its mouth. Good only over short distances, these glands can detect even a faint muscular twitch of an intended victim— even a faint heart beat—and guide the shark flawlessly toward its meal.

Yet, even with this array of high-tech detection equipment, sharks are instinctively cautious, almost timid. They tend to circle wide around the target, spiraling ever closer. The shark searches warily for unfamiliar creatures or swimming patterns. It probes for any hint of danger. If the vibration, smell, and look of a specific target are unfamiliar to the shark, it might well dart forward and brush past the new prey to see how it reacts before daring to attack.

Large sharks are brutal, vicious, and deadly. But they are not natural fighters. They do not want to endure struggle or combat to win a prized meal. They would rather wander off in search of an easier catch elsewhere.

Interestingly, sharks tend to explore the world with their mouths. It's called *test biting*—sort of like picking up an unknown object with your hands to study it more closely. Sharks are equipped with phenomenal hearing, smell, and electro-chemical sensors, and yet they feel they must hold things in their mouths in order to understand them. Scientists don't know why. Almost all great white "attacks" on humans have been test bites—ones that leave great ripping gashes, but ones in which the shark does not eat the victim.

Limited studies have shown that sharks are surprisingly smart. But scientists aren't sure just how smart. They may possess pack identity and loyalty. They may hunt in coordination like lionesses do and that's why they tend to gather in small, specific areas. They may have a social hierarchy and formal ways through which different generations interact. They may be faithful and gregarious. But scientists haven't been able to conduct the needed observational studies in the open ocean to find out.

Only a dozen researchers scattered across the world are currently studying great white sharks. At that rate, it will take decades to amass the necessary database to be able to understand and protect the king of the ocean from its one natural predator—humans. The research continues—as does the steep decline in great white populations. And great whites are the focus of far more research effort than is any other shark species.

— TOPICS FOR DISCUSSION AND PROJECTS

Here are activities, research topics, and discussion questions you can use to expand upon the key science concepts presented in this chapter.

Research and Discuss. Are shark populations rising or falling in the Earth's oceans? Focus on the big five shark species for human attacks: great white, tiger, bull, leopard, and hammerhead sharks. Chart their estimated worldwide populations over the past 200 years. Could you find accurate population estimates for these species? Why do you think we know so little about them? Why do you think scientists haven't conducted extensive studies of sharks?

What forces are pushing these large sharks toward extinction? What forces will help them survive? Sharks have survived on Earth for hundreds of millions of years. Why are they now struggling to survive?

Research and Discuss. Research one of the two large filter-feeding sharks (basking and whale sharks) and report on the population and life cycle information you are able to find. Were you surprised at how little information you found? Now research one of the small bay and estuarine sharks (there are a number of shark species less than two feet in length). Were you able to find much about the lives and population of these shark species?

An Activity. Mark on a U.S. map the locations of reported shark attacks in the past fifty years and use some code to indicate the species of shark involved in each attack. Prepare a second map showing great white shark sightings. Are they concentrated in a few areas? Is that because that's where the sharks were or because those are the only places observers were out looking to sight sharks.

Research and Discuss. Should we work to save great white sharks or let them become extinct? Search for arguments on both sides of this question. Why would scientists want to study and understand great white sharks? What benefits could the studies produce? List as many reasons as you can.

Research and Discuss. Diving with sharks is dangerous. Yet observational studies are essential if scientists are to accurately learn about shark behavior. How would you decide how much danger is acceptable during your own research? How do you decide how much risk and danger you will accept in your daily life?

An Activity. Coral reefs are unique marine environments and were mentioned as a territory of the oceans dominated by sharks. What is coral? What makes coral reefs such rich and densely populated habitats? What lives in, on, and around coral reefs? Why do they live *there*?

Prepare a map showing the location of major coral reefs around the world. See how many coral reefs you can locate. Can you think of any common factors in the environments at these locations that support the formation of coral and coral reefs? Are coral reefs expanding or shrinking? If you find that many are shrinking and dying, search for the reasons behind their demise.

Prepare a schematic map of one coral reef and the life that abounds there. What does a coral reef look like? What color is the coral and the water around the reef? What lives there? How big is the reef? What is the depth of water at your coral reef?

Research and Discuss. Sharks are one of the oldest predators on Earth. Shark species remarkably similar to today's large predator sharks existed long before dinosaurs first roamed the Earth. They have changed very little during the past 400 million years. Why do you think sharks have been so successful and have not had to evolve as most species have?

An Activity. Are sharks a major danger for humans visiting the beach? See if you can find statistics at your library or online to determine how many Americans die and are injured each year from each of the following dangers associated with a trip to the ocean. Prepare a chart to display your findings.

- Shark attacks.
- Drowning while swimming in the ocean.
- Boating accidents.
- Scuba diving accidents.
- Cuts from glass, metal, shells in the sand or on seaside rocks, or spiny urchins.
- Second- or third-degree sunburns.
- Stings by poisonous jellyfish.
- Automobile accidents driving to and from the beach.

Research and Discuss. Does anything prey on sharks? What controls shark populations and keeps them from growing unchecked as the human population is currently doing?

SUGGESTED READING

Arnold, Caroline. *Watch out for Sharks!* New York: Clarion Books, 1996.

Berger, Melvin. *What Do Sharks Eat for Dinner?* New York: Scholastic, 2001.

Blassingame, Wyatt. *Wonders of Sharks.* New York: Dodd, Mead, 1993.

Cerullo, Mary. *Sharks: Challengers of the Deep.* New York: Cobblehill Books, 1998.

———. *The Truth about Great White Sharks.* San Francisco: Chronicle Books, 2003.

Cook, Joseph. *The Nightmare World of the Shark.* New York: Dodd, Mead, 1998.

Copps, Dale. *Savage Survivor: 300 Million Years of the Shark.* Milwaukee, WI: Westwind Press, 1996.

Coupe, Sheena. *Sharks.* New York: Facts on File, 2000.

Davies, Nicolas. *Surprising Sharks.* Cambridge, MA: Candlewick Press, 2003.

Ferrari, Andrea. *Sharks.* Toronto: Firefly Books, 2002.

Gibbons, Gail. *Sharks.* New York: Holiday House, 1992.

Gourley, Catherine. *Sharks!: True Stories and Legends.* Brookfield, CT: Millbrook Press, 1996.

Haven, Kendall. *Close Encounters with Deadly Dangers.* Denver, CO: Libraries Unlimited, 1998.

Langley, Andrew. *The World of Sharks.* New York: Bookwight Press, 1988.

Lawrence, R. *Shark!: Nature's Masterpiece.* Shelburne, VT: Chapters Publications, 1994.

Maestro, Betsy. *A Sea Full of Sharks.* New York: Scholastic, 1996.

Markle, Sandra. *Outside and Inside Sharks.* New York: Athenuem Books for Young Readers, 1996.

Michael, Scott. *Reef Sharks of the World.* Monterey, CA: Challengers Books, 1998.

Parker, Steve, and Jane Parker. *The Encyclopedia of Sharks.* Toronto: Firefly Books, 2002.

Patent, Dorothy. *How Smart Are Animals?* San Diego: Harcourt Brace, 1999.

Perrine, Doug. *Sharks.* Stillwater, MN: Voyageur Press, 1995.

Sattler, Helen. *Fish Facts and Bird Brains.* New York: Lodestar Books, 1997.

———. *Sharks: The Super-Fish.* New York: Lothrop, Lee, and Shepard, 2000.

Sharth, Sharon. *Sharks and Rays.* New York: Franklin Watts, 2002.

Wexo, John. *Sharks.* Poway, CA: Wildlife Education, 2001.

Wilson, Lynn. *Sharks!* New York: Platt and Munk, 2002.

—— SUGGESTED READING FOR TEACHERS

Budker, Paul. *The Life of Sharks.* New York: Columbia University Press, 2001.

Clark, Eugenie. *Lady with a Spear.* New York: Harpers Publishing Co., 1953.

Clark, Ginger. *Sharks!* New York: Grosset and Dunlop, 2001.

Cole, Joanna. *Hungry, Hungry Shark.* New York: Random House, 1996.

Ellis, Richard. *Monsters of the Sea.* New York: Alfred A. Knopf, 1994.

Klimley, Pete. *The Secret Life of Sharks.* New York: Simon & Schuster, 2003.

MacQuitty, Miranda. *Shark.* New York: Alfred A. Knopf, 2002.

Mallory, Kenneth. *Swimming with Hammerhead Sharks.* Boston: Houghton Mifflin, 2001.

Wilson, Lynn. *Sharks!* New York: Platt and Munk, 1997.

Yount, Lisa. *Contemporary Women Scientists.* New York: Facts on File, 1994.

10 ···················· Ocean Mammals

——— MYTHS ABOUT OCEANIC MAMMALS

Why do air-breathing mammals live in the ocean? What are they doing there? Oceans are for fish. Land is for mammals and reptiles. But there they are: warm-blooded mammals cavorting in the seas—whales, seals, dolphins, porpoises, sea lions, walruses, manatees, and sea otters.

How did they get there? Why did they decide to live in the ocean instead of on land where mammals belong?

At the same time that humans have consistently slaughtered every marine mammal they could find, we have given some of these same creatures an exalted place in our mythologies. There are many stories about seal woman who can step out of their sealskin and become human. They are always kind, gentle, and wise. Whales are always mythically depicted as being intelligent, patient, and kind. (With a few fictional and more modern exceptions, like *Moby Dick*.)

Walrus appear in a few myths of several arctic cultures and always in the role of an oracle—one with cosmic understanding who dispenses wisdom to struggling humans. Sea lions, manatees, and otters never achieved central roles in myths. Otters cavort and romp in the oceans like jesters. They amuse us. For centuries they provided food and fur coats for us. But they never had a role as mythic characters.

Whales are different. Whales are central—even pivotal—to many myths. In these myths, man struggles to gain the insights and wisdom of the whale. Man can kill the whale, but man needs to learn from the whale. The whale in the ocean is often given the same attributes as the elephant on land—wisdom, long memory, patience, steadfastness, loyalty, and honor.

The myth that follows is typical of this group in its treatment of whales. Humans need to find love and to learn how to come together in peace. In the story, they are stuck without the help of a whale. The myth was given to me by storyteller Kevin Cordi, who received permission to use and adapt it from tribal elders.

"The Gift Giver," a Myth from the Pacific Northwest Yokut Tachi Tribe

Ships glide over the ocean. Fish dance through the ocean. But the depths of the oceans hold secrets only the whales know.

Once there lived a kind man in a small village on one side of the ocean. Though he lived alone, that man had a strong longing to seek the heart of another. He searched and he searched. His longing consumed his every thought and waking moment. But day after day and year after year he could not find the one that would heal his aching heart.

One day, as he strolled near the ocean's edge he heard the water call out to him—he *felt* the water call to him. He felt drawn to the water. As his feet touched the gentle waves, the man knew he heard a voice—a voice from far across the ocean. Though he could not make out any words, he knew he heard a beautiful female voice. He began to answer the voice. At first he simply wished and then he whispered his feelings and his longings across the ocean.

That whisper must have traveled far across the water because he heard a beautiful voice answer him. And now the words were as clear as the voices in his own mind, though the voice came from nowhere other than from far across the sea. And the words and the voice washed over him like soothing spring rain and made his heart smile light and happy for the first time in years.

From that day forward the man would whisper his wishes, wants, and desires across the waves for hours and hours at a time. Despite the work that had to be done he always made time for his lady across the water.

One sparkling morning, just as the Sun peaked above the glistening ocean, he rose early to tell his mysterious voice a special dream he had. However, when he arrived at the shore he found he was not alone. Near the water's edge floated a whale—a majestic creature that towered high above the man.

And the whale said, "I have heard your wishes, your wants, and your desires. I can help you."

But the man did not hear the whale's words. The man was thinking like a man—like a hunter—and saw the whale as meat and as something huge and mighty to be feared. The man was not armed and so could not attack. Therefore he fled.

But he had not spoken to his unknown love across the sea. So by the next day his heart lay heavy in his chest and he returned to the shore. Again he found the whale waiting for him.

The whale said, "If you will trust me and the ocean, I will carry you to see the one your heart longs for. I have heard your voice. I know your desire. I know your secret wish. Climb upon my back and I will take you to meet her."

But the man was afraid. "I can't trust a wild beast of the ocean. You'll eat me or drown me." And again he left.

But by the third day the man knew that his heart would break if he did not risk his very life to meet his distant love. When the invitation came to climb onto the whale's back, the man crawled up the side of the gigantic whale. His heart pounded with fear at the thought of crossing the ocean that was wider than all imagining on the back of a whale. But even louder, his heart roared with eager hope and anticipation.

The whale swam swift and true through the waves at incredible speed until it reached the other side of the ocean.

And there, standing on the shore, staring far out to sea, the man saw a woman. Her long black hair blew wild in the wind as she stood whispering her desires to the ocean.

The man recognized that beautiful voice and, with his heart racing so fast he could scarcely breathe, he answered her.

She squealed with delight and ran to embrace him. They held each other for long minutes before the words and questions and laughter tumbled from their mouths.

But then a man from her tribe saw the massive whale and a strange man holding the woman. Thinking the woman was in great danger, he cried out an alarm and threw a freshly carved spear. That spear pierced the side of the whale so that its entire body shuddered with the pain. Other men grabbed their spears and ran to the beach, hoping to kill both the whale and the man.

"Hurry man. Climb on my back, it is not safe here. I must return you to your village."

"But I *can't* leave yet," answered the man. "My love and I have only just met."

"Hurry man," bellowed the whale, "or we will both die."

The man wailed in bitter frustration and climbed onto the whale. In seconds they were deep in the bay and safe from the spears and arrows of the woman's tribesmen. The last sound the man heard before the shore disappeared below the horizon was the woman's sobbing cry of despair at their parting.

From that day on the man and the woman, despite the insistence of their tribes, refused to work, ate very little, and instead spent their time whispering their wants, wishes, and desires to each other across the ocean. After two long years, in the quiet of the night, the whale returned.

He approached the man who sat on the beach and said, "I have returned. Climb upon my back and I will take you to the one you love and you will be with her forever."

"But how?" demanded the man. "Her people will kill me if I go there, and my people will likely kill her or make her a slave if I bring her here."

"If you trust me," answered the whale, "I will show you where you can be together forever."

The man scrambled onto the whale's back and the whale raced through the endless ocean miles to the woman. When the man reached out his hand and called to the woman, she eagerly climbed upon the whale's back and sat content with her arm around the man who had filled her heart.

The whale swam to the middle of the ocean. No one but a whale knows where the exact middle of the ocean resides. And there the whale stopped, endless miles of desolate blue waves stretched in every direction.

"*This* is the only place where the two of you can be together."

Without words the man and woman held each other in their arms, joy and contentment on their faces.

The whale slowly rolled over on its side and the man and woman, in a firm embrace fell, fell happily to the bottom of the sea.

The whale paused at the spot, breathed deeply, and slowly swam away.

—— THE SCIENCE OF OCEANIC MAMMALS

The following beliefs are either directly stated or strongly implied in the presented myth. Here is what modern science knows about the aspects of the seas explained by each belief.

BELIEF: Ocean mammals started on land.

Here is the current best guess for how life evolved on this planet and how marine mammals wound up living in the sea. Scientists believe that life started in the oceans and later emerged from the sea as the result of an accident. A sudden drop in ocean level or a sudden rising of a stretch of land stranded some life form above the waterline. Or perhaps it was more gradual. Some intertidal plant species slowly adapted to being longer and longer out of water as it inched higher on the rocks and finally moved fully onto shore.

The first successful switch from sea to land was surely made by plants and it happened about 470 million years ago. It was probably by some species of seaweed that had already developed roots in order to cling to submerged coastal rocks, or some algae-like species that could get along in fresh water and moved higher on the rocks and dirt banks as moss.

Marine animals stranded on land with no plants to eat would have had to return to the sea for food. But once plants flourished on land, animals could follow. About 350 million years ago, some amphibian animals left the sea to live on land. Some of these developed into reptiles. Some reptiles evolved into mammals.

Sometime during the reign of dinosaurs (around 100 million years ago), something remarkable happened. A large land animal—an ancestor of modern whales—decided to return to the sea after living and developing on land for several hundreds of millions of years.

Those ancestors of whales freely roamed the Earth. They walked on four legs and had jaws and teeth. Presumably their favorite hunting ground grew to be the shallow bays and inlets that abounded along the coast. Fish and shellfish were probably more plentiful and easier to catch than land animals. Eventually, these ancestors of whales simply stayed in the water and learned to swim. Marine mammals are a recent life form on this planet. Seals and walruses are only 55 million years old, manatees only 40 million.

Millennia later, the forelegs of these animals became flippers for steering. The hind legs shrank to mere useless traces, vestiges of the legs that marine mammals had depended upon on land. But those leg bones can still be found in rudimentary form deep under the skin when a whale is cut up.

Seals, porpoises, otters, walruses, manatees, and sea lions presumably developed in the same way. But lungs are not as easy to change and evolve as are legs and flippers. None of the marine mammals have been able to develop the ability to "breathe" ocean water. All are still trapped along the surface, needing to poke their heads above water each time they need to breathe.

While life began in the seas and spread to land, ocean mammals have their roots on land and made a choice to move back into the sea—ei-

FIGURE 10.1 • Profiles of Marine Mammals

Blue Whale

Orca Whale

Sperm Whale

Manatee

Walrus

Porpoise

Sea Otter

Sea Lion

ther to avoid land predators or to take advantage of more plentiful ocean food supplies.

. . . .

BELIEF: Ocean mammals are superior to (at an advantage over) fish.

Science has found that there is no simple yes-or-no answer to this question. There are both plusses and minuses (advantages and disadvantages) to being a mammal living in the ocean. First the disadvantages. There are three and they are *huge* disadvantages.

Pressure. Air pressure at the surface of the ocean is 14.7 pounds of pressure per square inch (psi). That is the pressure of the air weighing down on your body. You have felt that pressure all your life and are used to it so that you are not even aware of it as you pace through your daily life.

Pressure increases rapidly under water so that the pressure at the bottom of the Pacific Ocean is 5,500 psi! That is enough to squeeze a block of solid wood to half its normal size. Why this massive pressure? It is because water is heavier (more dense) than air. Water weighs down and presses down on what is below it more than air does.

The problem is that air-breathing mammals fill their lungs with air. Air is a gas, and gasses are more susceptible to pressure and are much more easily compressed than water. The tremendous pressure of the ocean wants to crush the lungs, inner ears, sinuses, and other air-filled cavities of a mammal. Scuba divers and snorkelers feel this pressure painfully pressing in on their ears at depths as shallow as fifteen feet.

To protect themselves, mammals must either stay near the surface and avoid the pressure or develop stronger bones to protect their inner organs. Because food gathering requires marine mammals to dive to depths where the pressure is dangerous for their ears, they have had to evolve bones much thicker and denser than land-based mammals. The bones that protect a whale's ear canals are the densest bones on Earth, often weighing hundreds of pounds for the same size as a human bone that would weigh only a pound or two.

Body Temperature. Fish are cold blooded. Their circulating blood and bodies live at the temperature of the surrounding water. This scheme is amazingly efficient. A fish doesn't have to expend any energy trying to maintain a fixed body temperature.

Not so with mammals. Mammals have a body temperature much higher than the ocean water, which is constantly robbing heat from the mammal's body. Anyone who swims in a cold ocean knows that a person's body begins to stiffen, turn blue, and tremble from the cold after a few minutes of exposure. Ocean mammals face that problem every minute of every day.

Then how do ocean mammals survive the cold? Humans could not. Scuba divers have solved this problem by taking a cue from marine mammals. Divers wear wet suits—insulated layers that prevent cold water from reaching the body and stealing away its heat.

Thick fat layers called *blubber* lie just under the skin of marine mammals and surround them just as a wet suit surrounds and protects a diver. Blubber allows marine mammals to maintain their warm inner body temperature by insulating them from the ocean's cold. Still, marine mammals must eat almost ten times as much as an equal weight fish. Most of that food energy is used to produce heat to maintain the mammal's body temperature.

Breathing. Mammals breathe air, and air can only be found at the ocean's surface. Thus every marine mammal is forced to live on or near the ocean surface. In order to take each breath in their water-filled world, a mammal's head and nose must rise above the surface. They can't stay submerged where the food lies, but must bob endlessly up and down—up to breathe and down to eat. It wastes huge amounts of energy. But poor ocean mammals don't have any other choice. As a result, marine mammals have learned to hold their breath far longer than land-based mammals. Whales and seals can hold their breath for thirty to sixty minutes without strain.

Why do ocean mammals put up with such disadvantages that should make life at sea both miserable and more difficult for them than for any fish? We must also look at the advantages of being a marine mammal. There are three.

Intelligence. A warm-blooded circulatory system allows mammals to develop and maintain bigger brains. Marine mammals have the advantage of more intelligence. (See below.)

Speed. Warm muscles respond faster than cold. Marine mammals can swim faster than most cold-blooded fish. Some orcas and porpoise can top 40 miles per hour. Layers of body fat also allow marine mammals to develop a sleek, aerodynamic shape that aids in their quest for speed.

Flexibility. Except for whales, marine mammals have a real choice—stay in the water or waddle out and sit on land. When ocean predators (sharks) are near, mammals climb onto the land for safety. When land predators approach, marine mammals slide back into the water. Marine mammals—except for whales—must hug both the coastline and the surface in order to take advantage of this flexibility. They are forced to live along the thin edges of the oceans. But by accepting that limit, they gain a tremendous advantage by being able to choose between land and sea environments and avoid all predators.

Whales have given up the ability to crawl out onto land. In return, they have gained enormous size and the freedom to swim anywhere in the oceans that goes with being the biggest animals in the sea.

In summary, then, what do mammals gain by choosing to live in the sea and accepting the disadvantages they have to bear?

Food Supply. The coastal oceans have traditionally been a richer, denser ecosystem than those on adjacent land. The ocean can support more grazer fish and, thus, more predators.

Safety. Marine mammals' flexibility allows them to avoid both ocean and land predators that are stuck in one specific environment. Whales use their sheer size to create safety.

· ·

BELIEF: Ocean mammals are intelligent.

In the story, the whale was the one who understood the situation and formulated successful plans. The whale was the most intelligent being in the story. Other myths elevate marine mammals to similar lofty positions. But are they really that smart?

Studies have repeatedly shown that marine mammals are among the most intelligent animals on Earth. Orca, porpoise, dolphins, and seal are routinely trained to perform in circuses and marine theme parks. No one has trained salmon and flounders to do tricks. Many porpoises have learned to recognize and understand more than fifty words of spoken English. No human has ever been able to learn and understand even one word of porpoise.

Scientists who study animal behavior rank chimpanzees as the most intelligent animal on Earth (other than humans). Several species of small whale, dolphins, and porpoises are among the ten most intelligent animal species.

Sharks are probably the most intelligent fish species and many studies have been conducted (principally by Dr. Eugenie Clark in Florida) to demonstrate this shark intelligence and their ability to learn and correctly perform a variety of tasks. But no fish can hold a candle to the brain power of most marine mammal species.

— TOPICS FOR DISCUSSION AND PROJECTS

Here are activities, research topics, and discussion questions you can use to expand upon the key science concepts presented in this chapter.

An Activity. Let's demonstrate the effect of increased water pressure. For this activity you will need a tall, cylindrical plastic or metal can (46-ounce juice can or larger), a ruler, a nail (at least two and a half inches long), a hammer, masking tape, water, and a large sink in which to work.

With your teacher's supervision, use the hammer and nail to make a row of four holes in the side of the can. With the can on its side, measure and mark a spot one inch from the bottom of the can for the first hole. The second hole will be placed one inch above the first. The third will be one inch above the second, and the fourth will be one inch above the third. Cover all four holes with masking tape.

Set the can at the edge of the sink and fill it with water. Quickly remove all four pieces of tape and watch the streams of water squirting form each hole. Which stream shoots the farthest? The greater the water pressure, the greater the force pushing water out of the hole and the farther it will squirt.

Research and Discuss. What is a mammal? What is the difference between a mammal and a fish? Between a mammal and a reptile? What are the advantages and disadvantages of dividing animals into these categories? Do those three categories include all of the animal kingdom? What other groups of animals are there?

Research and Discuss. Human hunters have always viewed marine mammals as an excellent source of food. Why else have humans hunted and killed marine mammals? What other products do people get from these animals? Are there other reasons that have driven humans to kill marine mammals?

Canadian seals and Pacific sea otters were (in the first half of the twentieth century) slaughtered because they competed with human fishermen for the same food sources. Porpoises and seals are often killed in fishing nets. Most fishermen say, "Good riddance." When marine mammals compete with humans, do you think it is justifiable to kill the mammals? Research this phenomenon and search for reasons on both sides of the issue.

Research and Discuss. Both the story and the science discussion above talk about animal intelligence and claim that marine mammals are intelligent. Research intelligence. What is it? What does it mean to be intelligent? Research the intelligence of marine mammals. Which are most intelligent? Least? How does anyone know?

An Activity. Measuring animal intelligence is a difficult task. You can't ask an animal a series of questions and grade its answers. How do scientists evaluate animal intelligence?

In small groups (three to four students per group) make a list of what you think are the five smartest animals. Next to each animal's name, say why you think that animal is so intelligent. What do they do that makes you think they are intelligent? Compare lists between groups and see if you all used the same reasons (factors) for deciding which animals are intelligent.

Research how scientists conduct animal intelligence tests and then write down two factors you think are the most important in determining animal intelligence. As a class, vote for the two factors from these lists that the group thinks are the most important. How could you measure these two factors you have chosen? Is there a test you could conduct to see which animals perform best at these intelligence factors?

Make a list of all household pets owned by members of your class. Your goal is to use one of the two intelligence factors your class selected to see which of these species of pets will be crowned the most intelligent pet of the class.

First, you must design, and agree upon, a test to measure this factor. The test must be simple enough so that you can all to do it at home with your own pets. But it must be hard enough to really test the intelligence of your pets. Search through the library and Internet for tests that other researcher have used. You must also decide how to tell when a pet is successful at this test. Is it speed, accuracy, how often they do the test correctly?

After completing the test, review the results for each pet. What made conducting the test hard? Did your pets cooperate? Did they try to do the test? Do you think they knew they were being tested? What does that tell you about their intelligence? Did all the members of any one pet species do equally well on your test? Is it hard to tell which pets did best? Which pet won the title of most intelligent class pet?

Look at your class's results. Could you have come to the same conclusion without a test? Could you have figured out which was most intelligent just by observing their natural behavior? Observe ants, flies, and snails. Which do you think is most intelligent? Why?

An Activity. Make a chart of ocean animals that crawled onto land. Make another list of land animals that later crawled back into the sea. Include mammals, reptiles, and insects in your lists. Are there any animals that have changed from land to sea or from sea to land in the last million years?

Research the African hippopotamus. It spends most of its life under water, sitting in the soft mud of shallow rivers. Has the hippo always spent this much time in the water? Do modern hippos spend more time in the water than they did 2,000 years ago? 100,000 years ago? Might they eventually become another land mammals that shifted back into a water environment? What do you think, and why?

Research and Discuss. How have marine mammal populations changed over the past 500 years? Pick three species of marine mammal and research their population numbers. How have they changed? Why? If their populations have dramatically dipped, how much of that dip can be attributed to human activity? How are the populations of your three chosen species forecast to change over the next fifty years? The next 100 years?

Research and Discuss. How has ocean pollution affected marine mammals? Does it affect them in the same ways it affects humans? What kinds of pollution affect marine mammals the most? (You may consider noise pollution as well as the many chemical and solid pollutants dumped and spilled into the ocean.)

SUGGESTED READING

Berta, Annalisa. *Marine Mammals: Evolutionary Biology.* San Diego: Elsevier Science, 1999.

Burton, Robert. *The Life and Death of Whales.* London: Andre Deutch, 2000.

Cahill, Tim. *Dolphins.* Washington, DC: National Geographic Society, 2003.

Carwardine, Mark. *Whales, Dolphins, and Porpoises.* New York: DK Publishers, 1999.

Corrigan, Pat. *Whales.* New York: T & N Children's Press, 2001.

Ellis, Richard. *The Book of Whales.* New York: Alfred A. Knopf, 1989.

———. *Men and Whales.* New York: Alfred A. Knopf, 1991.

Facklam, Margery. *What Does the Crow Know?* San Francisco: Sierra Club Books for Young Readers, 1997.

Kalman, Bobbie, ed. *What Is a Marine Mammal?* New York: Crabtree Publishing, 1999.

Knudtson, Peter. Orca: *Visions of the Killer Whale.* Toronto: Douglas and McIntyre, 2004.

Landau, Elaine. *Ocean Mammals*. New York: Scholastic, 1998.

Mason, Adrienne, ed. *Oceans*. Tonawanda, NY: Kids Can Press, 1999.

McClung, Robert. *Thor, Last of the Sperm Whales*. New York: Morrow, 1991.

Nichollson, Sue. *Ocean Explorers*. New York: Scholastic, 2002.

Patent, Dorothy. *How Smart Are Animals?* San Diego: Harcourt Brace, 1998.

Perrin, William, ed. *Encyclopedia of Marine Mammals*. San Diego: Elsevier Science, 2002.

Reeves, Randal, ed. *National Audubon Society Guide to Marine Mammals*. New York: Alfred A. Knopf, 2002.

Rustad, Martha. *Manatees*. Mankato, MN: Capstone Press, 2001.

Sattler, Helen. *Fish Facts and Bird Brains*. New York: Lodestar Books, 1994.

Savage, Stephen. *Animals of the Ocean*. Chicago: Raintree Publications, 1998.

Scheffer, Victor. *Little Calf*. New York: Scribner, 1970.

———. *The Year of the Whale*. New York: Scribner, 1969.

Taylor, Dave. *Endangered Ocean Mammals*. New York: Crabtree Publishing, 1998.

Whitehead, Hal. *Voyage to the Whale*s. Post Mills, VT: Chelsea Green Publication Company, 1997.

Yount, Lisa. *Contemporary Women Scientists*. New York: Facts on File, 1994.

—— SUGGESTED READING FOR TEACHERS

Cohat, Yves. *Whales: Giants of the Seas.* New York: Harry Abrams, 2001.

Committee on Potential Impacts of Amblen. *Ocean Noise and Marine Mammals.* Washington, DC: National Academy Press, 2004.

Ellis, Richard. *The Book of Whales.* New York: Alfred A. Knopf, 1995.

Emberlin, Diane. *Contributions of Women to Science.* Minneapolis, MN: Dillion Press, 1992.

Hand, Douglas. *Gone Whaling.* New York: Simon & Schuster, 2001.

Heyney, John. *Masters of the Ocean Realm.* Seattle: University of Washington Press, 1998.

Orr, Robert. *Marine Mammals.* Berkeley: University of California Press, 1999.

Reynolds, John, ed. *Biology of Marine Mammals.* Washington, DC: Smithsonian Institute Press, 1999.

Ridgeway, Sam. *Handbook of Marine Mammals.* San Diego: Elsevier Science, 1998.

Slijpin, Everhard. *Whales.* Ithaca, NY: Cornell University Press, 1999.

Twiss, John, ed. *Conservation and Management of Marine Mammals.* Washington, DC: Smithsonian Institute Press, 1999.

Utah State University Department of Wildlife. *Sperm Whale Population Analysis.* Washington, DC: Marine Mammal Commission, 1997.

Whitehead, Hal. *Sperm Whales.* Chicago: University of Chicago Press, 2003.

11 .... Origins of Fish

MYTHS ABOUT THE ORIGINS OF FISH

Ocean waters were created by rain and volcanic venting. But how did that vast expanse of water come to be populated by the great variety of fishes that exist today? There is far greater variety of shapes and sizes of fish in the ocean than for animals on land. Shellfish, sea horses, fin fish, swordfish, jellyfish, eels, stingrays, octopus, flying fish, electric fish, starfish, sponges, sea cucumbers, urchins, sea snakes, squid, worms, corals, sea birds (penguins), plankton, sharks—presented in a rainbow of every imaginable color. Some bold and bright. Some soft and muted. Some able to create their own chemical lights. Some electrified as if filled with batteries. It's as if Nature decided to let her imagination and paint brush go wild in the oceans. Compared to the oceans, land creatures are pretty dull and ordinary.

Where did this vast variety come from? Did it just happen, or was it somehow planned? The teeming world under the oceans seemed a bewildering mystery to early man—especially because humans depend on the seas and this assortment of fish for food. It was the perfect topic for mythic stories.

A myth from the African country of Benin begins with an agreement between Moon and Sun. But Moon tricks Sun into throwing all his children into the ocean. Once the Sun realizes it is a trick, he finds to his dismay that he can't take his children back out of the sea without having them die. The children of the Sun become sea dwellers. Children of the Moon become land dwellers. Sun becomes forever angry at Moon and chases her around the sky.

In an Indian story, crab, frog, shrimp, octopus, and minnow are all friends and shaped alike. The other four play a trick on crab during which he volunteers to cast his body parts one by one into the cook pot so that there will be meat for the others to eat. The others laugh so hard that they double over with laughter. They laugh for days on end. After they stop they find that they have permanently changed into the shape they held while laughing and crab is given a hard shell to protect him from his friends.

A Chinese story explains why the jellyfish has no bones. Octopus, a councilor in the king's court, was jealous of the honest, simple, popular, and very speedy—but very gullible—jellyfish. Octopus tricked jellyfish into volunteering for an impossible task. When jellyfish failed, octopus talked the king into having jellyfish beaten (during which every one of his bones was broken). In the end, the princess exposes octopus's treachery. The king banishes octopus to a solitary and lonely life slinking along the ocean floor while jellyfish (still with no bones) becomes everyone's favorite sea dweller. So now jellyfish can float slowly through the water and not be bothered by other sea creatures.

The myth that follows comes from the Maori people of New Zealand and explains how all the fish were first given their unique shapes and characteristics—and does it wrapped in a myth of betrayal, battle, and revenge.

"The Battle of the Fishes," a Myth from the Maori of New Zealand

The tears ran in streams down the woman's cheeks and stained her dress as she sat alone in her hut. Her husband had left her and she did not know where he had gone.

She asked the trees that grew tall and could see far across the forest. But the trees were silent. The stream that tumbled near their hut was enchanted and would give her no answer. The walls of their hut would not tell her, though she was sure that they had heard her husband talk and knew where he had gone.

Only the calabash from which he drank took any pity on her. "Do not grieve," it said. "Break me on the floor, gather up the pieces, and take me with you. I will then show you where he went."

At first the woman was reluctant to break so fine a calabash. But it insisted and so she thanked the calabash and dashed it onto the floor. It broke into a shattered jigsaw of pieces. The woman carefully picked up each piece, placed them gingerly into a basket, and set out.

The broken calabash told her the path to follow. She went on until she came to the bank of the enchanted stream. "Cross the stream here," the calabash pieces told her. As she waded through the cold and fast-flowing current, the water secretly crept into her basket and soaked the pieces of the calabash. It would speak no more.

The woman returned to her hut, tears again flowing down her face. There were dozens of paths through the forest and under the trees. Without guidance, there was no way she could tell which one to follow.

In the dark night her heart filled with bitter sadness because her husband had left her and frustration because no one would show her the way to go. Slowly, as she sat with knees drawn rocking to and fro, her sadness turned to anger.

In the distance, she heard the booming of ocean waves breaking upon the shore. The booming seemed to match her own growing anger and she decided to ask Tangaroa, the God of the Sea, for his help in avenging the wrong that had been done to her.

Like a wild creature of the woods, she slipped between the trees in the dim moonlight and reached the pale sand. Arms outstretched, she lifted her face to the stars. "Hear my prayer, oh Tangaroa, ruler of the sea. Great wrong has been done to me by my husband who left me and by the men who hide him from me. Comfort me, great Tangaroa, by destroying these evil ones."

Tangaroa needed little encouragement to make war upon the subjects of his brother, the land. In a voice like thunder he called to his people, the fishes. Quickly they responded and came to him, every one. Great fish and small fish, they all clustered about their god, Tangaroa. Each fish wore the plain gray livery of the children of Ika-tere. Every one of them was built in the same shape. Only in size did they vary, from Tohorta, the whale, down to tiny Inanga, the bait fish.

Like a great army these fish swam to shore and to the coastal village where the errant husband was living.

In the lead of this army swam the small pilot fish and reef fishes. In the rear swam the mighty whales whose huge bodies could act as a impassible wall to stem any rush of smaller fish who might flee at the onslaught of the Maoris.

The army reached the shore and climbed out onto the sand. They crashed through the undergrowth of the forest calling out their cry for the husband to come to justice. Their wet, shining bodies lumbered on, trampling grass and bush.

Presently they heard wild cries of alarm up ahead. Then they heard the pounding of countless drums and the battle cries of the Maori as the land people gathered to defend themselves.

All day long the dreadful battle raged. The Gurnard reef fish stormed the palisades of the land people and many of them were killed so that they were dyed red with their own blood—even as they are to this very day. The chief of the black perch tribe followed close behind, leading his warriors in support of the Gurnard, until every one of his warriors was covered in the dried blood of the advance.

Tribe after tribe of fish hurled themselves into the battle. As the sun slid low in the western sky, they saw the dead bodies of their comrades all around them and the little fish were frightened. They turned back and fled into the cool shadows of the trees where Tangaroa and his great warriors waited in reserve.

When Tangaroa saw the little fishes retreat in panic, he bellowed out his orders. The whales lurched forward. Trees were tossed left and right like leaves blown by the wind as the whales stomped into the battle.

As one, the line of mighty whales fell upon the walls of the land men's stronghold. The palisades cracked and splintered with the whales attack. The walls fell with crashes that shook the ground.

The defenders who were not crushed fled in terror and victory was won. The dwellers of the sea had defeated the land people. Triumph belonged to Tangaroa the Sea God.

The next day Tangaroa stood by his throne in his ocean home. His victorious army swam around him in a great circle shouting their war chants and giving praise to Tangaroa. As each tribe of his army swam past, Tangaroa gave it a boon to mark that tribe's contribution to victory.

The little Gurnards were given the honorable badge of their faithfulness to wear forever, the rich red of the blood of the brave fish that had led the army to war.

Patiki the flounder had been first across the land dwellers' walls and had raided their living huts. He had seen there a boy's toy and wished to be forever shaped like a kite.

Takeke, the swordfish, proudly bore a spear under his fin that he had captured from an enemy chief and asked that he might wear it on his head.

Whai, the stingray, too, carried a captured spear, one with a double row of barbs at its point, and this he wanted to carry at the end of his tail.

Eliki, the squid, had fought bravely in hand-to-hand combat and wished for long arms so that next time he would win more easily.

Tohorta, the giant whale, said that he wanted to remember the victory he won under the blue sky, and Tangaroa painted his top forever blue as a rememberance.

Last of all came Araara the Trevally, bearing a white cape that he had taken from the man who had left his wife. The cape was splattered with bright red stains of the man's blood and this became the garment that the Trevally would proudly wear forever.

So, in this way, did Tangaroa avenge the wrong that had been done. So, in this way, did he give the fishes their wonderful shapes and colors. To this day, the descendents of those fish still wear the proud scars and insignia that were won on the day that the fishes defeated men.

—— THE SCIENCE OF THE ORIGINS OF FISH

The following beliefs are either directly stated or strongly implied in the presented myth. Here is what modern science knows about the aspects of the seas explained by each belief.

BELIEF: The characteristics of the various fish were given to them by a god.

What does it mean to talk about the characteristics of fish? In general, we can focus on seven characteristics: size, shape, diet, habitat, color, abilities, and behavioral patterns. (Said differently, What does it look like? What does it eat? Where does it live? and What does it do?)

Each of these characteristics evolves over time to increase the chances of each species' survival. Englishman Charles Darwin first proposed the theory of evolution. With minor modification, it is still the prevailing belief to describe the history of animal development. A fish develops the habit of eating one particular food source. Over eons, that fish will tend to evolve physically to be better able to catch that food source.

On land, birds develop beak shapes that are best able to collect the seeds, nuts, or bugs that that particular bird prefers to eat. The same thing happens in the ocean. Over time (tens and hundreds of thousands of years) each species settles into a specific niche in order to survive. It develops physical characteristics and behavioral patterns that help it find food and avoid predators. It picks a habitat—a place to live, such as a coral reef, the deep ocean floor, open ocean, and so forth—that will give it a better chance to survive.

Over time, several species may compete for the same niche. One typically survives there. The other evolves and adapts to a new niche or drifts toward extinction. As the environment changes, each species must adapt and evolve. New predators move in and existing species must find new defensive strategies or be eaten.

Life in the ocean is a continuous struggle. Each individual and each species tries to eat and not be eaten, to expand its territory, to adapt and search for new strategies that give it an advantage over its competitors, to evolve into a more efficient organism in order to survive for another generation.

In developing their individual strategies, some sea creatures decided to hug the bottom and not swim at all: starfish, anemones, clams, worms, coral, mussels, sponges, oysters, abalone, crab, octopus. Some developed ways to swim without fins and flukes: jellyfish, sea snakes, stingrays, seahorse, squid, eel, viper fish. But most of the inhabitants of the sea are fish that use fins and tail flukes to get around.

Some ocean dwellers develop shells as defensive armor. Some rely on speed. Some are armed with deadly poison. One species of fish has long front fins it can use as wings and fly for as far as sixty feet through the air to avoid predators. Some develop razor-sharp teeth and rely on aggression. Grunion swim up onto the beach to lay their eggs in the sand so that other fish can't eat their eggs before they hatch. Each fish develops a set of characteristics that help it survive or else it drifts toward extinction.

WHAT TYPES OF OCEAN DWELLERS ARE THERE?

There are three types of living organisms in the ocean: *benthos* (animals and plants that live attached to the ocean floor; *nektos* (animals that swim—fish, turtles, penguines, sea snakes, etc.); and *plankton* (plants and small animals that float in the water or swim weakly). There are more than 250,000 known species in the oceans. Best current estimates say that there are between 1 and 10 million species in the ocean that have not yet been discovered. Most of these are believed to live in the deep oceans or along the ocean floor.

As is true for terrestrial ecosystems, aquatic ecosystems depend on plants as the supporting base for every living organism in the system. All plants that live in the ocean and are capable of photosynthesis are called *algae*.

Algae can be categorized by the kind of chlorophyll they contain to convert the Sun's light into plant matter (red algae, green algae, and brown algae). Algae may also be divided into those plants that are attached to the bottom (benthos, including seaweeds, sponges, and kelps) and those that float free in the water (plankton, called phytoplankton).

Some kelp grow as forests of towering stems that can rise seventy to eighty feet to reach the sunlight at the surface. Some seaweeds are stubby and tenacious plants that cling to coastal rocks and withstand the pounding of crashing waves. There are also many varieties of phytoplankton (microscopic floating ocean plants). Diatoms and dinoflagelates are the most common types. But hundreds of phytoplankton species grow in the surface layers of the world's oceans and estuaries.

There are also planktonic animals (zooplankton), microscopic ocean bugs. Zooplankton eat phytoplankton. The two most common of the many varieties of zooplankton are copepods and krill. Many small fish eat zooplankton. So do large filter feeders such as blue whales and basking sharks. Larger fish eat smaller fish.

Phytoplankton can only grow where there is adequate sunlight and chemical nutrients. Phytoplankton grow in the top several hundred feet of the ocean and especially in areas where nutrient-rich bottom water wells up to the surface. Small fish will concentrate where plankton thrive. Larger fish want to stay near, but not so near that they become easy targets for larger predators. Often larger fish will live lower in the water column to hide from predators and rise up once or twice a day to feed on plankton or on smaller fish.

Life in the ocean is wondrously diverse and wonderfully inventive. Different critters, different strategies for survival, different niches to fill. Yet all have one thing in common: They struggle to ensure the continued (and enhanced) survival of their species. The belief is wrong. The characteristics of fish species evolved, slowly, over long stretches of time to help each individual species survive and thrive.

BELIEF: Sea dwellers can defeat (and have defeated) land dwellers.

Certainly great white sharks, whales, giant squid, large octopuses, and saltwater crocodiles are ferocious and fearsome when met in one-on-one combat in the ocean. But on a larger scale, no sea creature is a match for humans. We have used our technology to hunt, catch, kill, and decimate most of the populations that live in the sea. For every one shark that has ever taken a bite out of a person, well over a million people have eaten shark.

Fishing records from the eighteenth century show that five- to six-foot-long lobsters were regularly caught around New York City and that the local waters were thick with shrimp, crab, oysters, and "fish of all varieties." Lobsters are now a rare catch in the area and rarely live long enough to grow more than one foot in length. Fishing boats have to travel out into the ocean or well into Long Island Sound to reach good fishing grounds. Those areas closer to the city have been fished out and polluted.

But beyond fishing (and over-fishing), humans dump pesticides, fertilizers, toxic wastes, sewage, garbage, and other pollutants into the ocean. Top open-ocean predator fish (swordfish, sharks, and tuna) are often tainted with heavy concentrations of mercury (a well-established poison). Thousands of acres of coastal waters are off limits for shell fishing because of the pollutant levels.

Humans also tend to destroy essential coastal habitat. Salmon runs on both coasts of the United States have been dramatically reduced and are continuously threatened by habitat destruction and stream alteration. Landfills along estuaries and bays destroy critical habitat for primary production (essential to support the entire ecosystem). High-powered ship engines and underwater sonar systems damage marine mammal inner ears and lead to massive whale beachings.

In the myth, sea dwellers defeated dwellers of the land. However, the reality is that we land dwellers are destroying the sea dwellers at an alarming rate. If this really were a war, it would be one that land dwellers would be wise not to win. We depend on the sea far more than the sea dwellers depend on the land. Were we to win the war and destroy the sea dwellers, it would lead to our own destruction as well.

. . . .

BELIEF: There are no remaining mysteries in the world of fish.

The myth seems to say that once the fish were given their specific characteristics, that was it. Nothing else changed. The oceans have been the same ever since and we know all that there is to know about the oceans.

Is that true? Absolutely not.

The only constant in the oceans is change. Water conditions change. Populations change. The oceans are in perpetual flux. They are also relatively unknown to humans. We humans have tramped over the land and studied the land for thousands of years. We understand the history of land, the populations that inhabit the land, and the dynamics of the ecosystems on land.

Not so for the oceans. Ocean science is a relatively new field of science. It is harder (and much more expensive) to get onto the ocean than it is to get onto the land in order to conduct a study. It is remarkably difficult and expensive to study the deep oceans and the ocean floor. So, relatively few studies have been undertaken.

The best current estimate is that 95% of ocean bottom-dwelling species have not yet been discovered. There is plenty of evidence that mysteries and marvelous discoveries still await us in the ocean realm. Several years ago, a previously unknown species of fish with real, working legs invaded Maryland coastal freshwater pools along the Chesapeake Bay. A very aggressive predator, it threatened to wipe out native species. Biologists quickly discovered that they couldn't trap this fish in isolated ponds and waterways because this fish can walk across hundreds of yards of land to next body of water!

Another fish with legs, the coelacanth, was an ugly blue fish with four legs that flourished 60 million years ago (according to fossil records). It officially became extinct 18 million years ago. (Coelacanths stopped appearing in the fossil record.) Then, in December 1938, a fisherman netted one alive and full grown off Capetown, South Africa, in 150 feet of water—five feet long, bright blue, with a big ugly head. Scientists rushed to South Africa to try to catch another. One South African professor of oceanography spent fourteen years trying before he finally caught one in 1952 just off a small island northwest of Madagascar. Since then more than twenty have been caught. Where had the coelacanth been hiding for almost 20 million years?

The *Galatea* expedition in 1988 used deep-sea submersibles to explore the Marianas Trench in the South Pacific and brought up a primitive mollusk that drifted past their submersible. The last known specimen of this particular mollusk had been petrified 400 million years ago. For 400 million years it dropped out of the fossil record, but then it suddenly reappeared!

Great mysteries remain under the ocean waves. There is life at depth in the seas we have never been able to study, mysteries we are not yet even aware of, and answers to evolution and the development of life on this planet. They all lie down there, waiting, if we are willing to venture down and find them.

— TOPICS FOR DISCUSSION AND PROJECTS

Here are activities, research topics, and discussion questions you can use to expand upon the key science concepts presented in this chapter.

Research and Discuss. At the end of the Maori myth, each animal is given a specialty, a niche. The science discussion above mentions niches. What is a niche? How do niches figure into the field of ecology? What does "having a niche" mean? Do humans have niches?

Research and Discuss. What is the theory of evolution? What does it say? What does it mean? How did Charles Darwin develop the theory? Can you find examples in the fish world of evolution in action?

An Activity. This chapter emphasizes the great variety of shapes and colors of the inhabitants of the fish world. Make a chart showing the different kinds of body shapes for creatures that live in the sea. How many different basic body shapes can you find? How many specific examples of each general body shape can you find?

Research and Discuss. How many fish live in the sea? Research population estimates for the total number. Can you find information about how the total fish population has changed over the past 100 years? Over the past 1,000 years? Over the past 1 million years? What are the main causes for any changes you find?

An Activity. As a class make a list of as many commercial fisheries as you can (tuna, salmon, crab, lobster, mackerel, jack, smelt, whale, etc.). Consult the library and the Internet for help in compiling this list. Have each student pick one fishery to research.

Research the following information for your fishery:

- Most recent annual catch (both United States and worldwide).

- Products this fish is used for.

- The equipment fishermen use to catch fish in this fishery.

- The location of prime fishing grounds for this fishery.

- Changes in the annual catch over the past twenty years.

- Government-imposed limits and regulations that control fishing for this fish species.

- Forecasts for future species population and catch levels.

- Population changes for this species over the past 1,000 years.

Make a scale drawing or model of your fish species to accompany the information you report.

Do you think we have over-fished this fish species? Is your fish species now contaminated with pesticides, mercury, and other major toxins and pollutants? Is that affecting catch levels and the usefulness of this fish?

Research and Discuss. Has ocean pollution affected commercial fish species? Has it affected plankton and coral? What do common pollutants do to plankton populations?

SUGGESTED READING

Cavandish, Marshall. *Aquatic Life of the World.* New York: Marshall Cavandish Company, 2001.

Demuth, Pat. *Way Down Deep: Strange Ocean Creatures.* New York: Grosset and Dunlap, 1999.

Erickson, Jon. *Marine Geology: Undersea Landforms and Life Forms.* New York: Facts on File, 1996.

Fowler, Allan. *Life in a Tide Pool.* New York: Scholastic Library, 1997.

Green, Edmund. *World Atlas of Coral Reefs.* Berkeley: University of California Press, 2002.

Karleskint, George. *Introduction to Marine Biology.* Minneapolis, MN: Brooks Cole, 1997.

Kent, Peter. *Hidden Under the Sea.* New York: Dutton Children's Books, 2001.

Littlefield, Cindy. *Awesome Ocean Science.* Nashville, TN: Ideal Publications, 2001.

Mason, Andrienne, ed. *Oceans.* Tonawanda, NY: Kids Can Press, 1997.

Morgan, Sally. *Ocean Life.* Phoenix, AZ: Sterling Publications, 2001.

Norris, Paul. *Aquaman's Guide to the Oceans.* New York: DK Publishers, 2004.

Parker, Steve. *Ocean Life.* Edison, NJ: Chartwell Books, 2001.

Reseck, John. *Marine Biology.* New York: Prentice Hall, 1996.

Ruth, Helen. *How to Hide an Octopus: And Other Sea Creatures.* New York: Grosset and Dunlap, 1999.

Savage, Stephen. *Animals of the Ocean*. Chicago: Raintree Publications, 1998.

Scott, Michael. *A Pocket Guide to Marine Fishes*. Neptune City, NJ: TFH Publications, 2001.

Swanson, Diane. *Safari Beneath the Sea*. Ontario, Canada: Whitecap Books, 1997.

Talbot, Frank, ed. *Under the Sea*. New York: Time-Life Books, 1998.

Waller, Geoffrey. *Sea Life: A Complete Guide*. Washington, DC: Smithsonian Press, 2001.

Wood, Lawson. *Reef Fishes*. New York: McGraw-Hill, 2000.

—— SUGGESTED READING FOR TEACHERS

Castro, Peter. *Marine Biology*. New York: McGraw-Hill, 2004.

Doris, Ellen. *Marine Biology*. New York: Thames & Hudson, 2003.

Ellis, Richard. *The Empty Ocean: Plundering the World's Marine Life*. Washington, DC: Island Press, 2003.

Kelly, Laurie. *Oceanography and Marine Biology*. Boca Raton, FL: CRC Press, 2004.

Levinton, Jeffry. *Marine Biology*. New York: Oxford University Press, 2001.

Norse, Elliot, ed. *Global Marine Biological Diversity*. Washington, DC: Island Press, 2003.

Nybakken, James. *Marine Biology*. New York: Benjamin Cummings, 2000.

Parfit, Michael. "Diminishing Returns: Exploiting the Ocean's Bounty." *National Geographic*, November 1995, 2–37.

Sales, Peter, ed. *Coral Reef Fishes*. San Diego: Elsevier Science, 2002.

Appendix: General Oceanography Web Sites and References

The search term "oceanography" produces over 3 million hits on each of the three major search engines. There are eighty university graduate degree programs in oceanography and 135 undergraduate programs. More than a dozen federal governmental agencies and more than thirty state-level agencies study, regulate, and control the coastal oceans. Each has its own Web page that describes and reports on their research and studies. There are literally thousands of valuable, reliable, information-filled sites on the Web. The few sites listed below cover a wide spectrum of oceanographic science fields and are some of the best and most dependable.

American Cetacean Society. *www.acsonline.org*.

American Oceans Campaign. *www.americanoceans.org*.

Caribbean Conservation Corp. *www.csc.noaa.gov/cmfp*.

Marine Conservation Biology Institute. *www.mcbi.org*.

Monterey Bay Aquarium. *www.mbayaq.org*.

NASA Oceanographic Sciences. *http://oceans.nasa.gov*.

National Oceanic and Atmospheric Administration. *www.nos.noaa.gov*.

Ocean Conservancy. *www.oceanconservancy.org.*

Oceanographic Society. *www.tos.org.*

Oceanography Resources Page. *www.esdim.noaa.gov.*

Reef Quest Center for Shark Research. *www.elasmo-research.org/education.*

Scripps Oceanic Institute. *http://sio.ucsd.edu.*

Scripps Oceanographic Library. *http://scilib.ucsd.edu.*

Smithsonian Institution. *www.si.edu.*

Smithsonian Museum of Natural History. *http://sewifs.gsfc.nasa.gov.*

Woods Hole Oceanographic Institute. *www.whoi.edu.*

Woods Hole Research Center. *www.whrc.org.*

World Wide Web Virtual Library of Oceanography. *www.mth.uea.uk/ocean/vl.*

———— GENERAL OCEANOGRAPHY BOOK REFERENCES

Andrews, Tamra. *Legends of the Earth, Sea, and Sky.* Santa Barbara, CA: ABC-CLIO, Inc., 1998.

Berger, Melvin, and Gilda Berger. *The Blue Planet.* New York: Scholastic, 2001.

————. *What Makes an Ocean Wave?* New York: Scholastic, 2000.

Borgese, Elizabeth, ed. *Ocean Frontiers: Explorations by Oceanographers.* New York: Harry Abrams, 2002.

Broad, William. *The Universe Below.* New York: Simon & Schuster, 1999.

Byath, Andrew, and Alastair Fothergit. *The Blue Planet: A Natural History of the Oceans.* New York: DK Publishers, 2001.

Carson, Rachel. *The Sea Around Us.* New York: Oxford University Press, 2003.

Collard, Sneed. *Deep Sea Floor.* Watertown, MA: Charlesbridge Publications, 2003.

Corfield, R. M. *The Silent Landscape.* Washington, DC: Joseph Henry Press, 2001.

Day, Trevor. *Oceans.* New York: Facts on File, 1999.

Doris, Ellen. *Marine Biology.* New York: Thames & Hudson, 2003.

Earle, Sylvia. *Atlas of the Deep Oceans.* Washington, DC: National Geographic Soceity, 2001.

Elder, Danny, ed. *The Random House Atlas of the Oceans.* New York: Random House, 1998.

Groves, Don. *The Oceans: A Book of Questions and Answers.* New York: John Wiley, 1999.

Hanson, Neil. *The Curtain of the Sea.* New York: John Wiley, 1999.

Kerwood, Robin. *The Sea.* Milwaukee, WI: Gareth Stevens Publisher, 1998.

Kunzin, Robert. *The Restless Sea.* New York: Norton, 1999.

Lambert, David. *Kingfisher Young People's Book of the Ocean.* New York: Kingfisher Books, 1997.

Leier, Manfred, ed. *World Atlas of the Oceans.* Tonawanda, NY: Firefly Books, 2001.

Littlefield, Cindy. *Awesome Ocean Science!* Charlotte, VT: Williamson Publishers, 2002.

Markle, Sandra. *Pioneering Ocean Depths.* New York: Atheneum, 1996

Mason, Adrienne, ed. *Oceans.* Tonawanda, NY: Kids Can Press, 1999.

Matsen, Brad. *Planet Ocean: Life, the Sea, and the Fossil Record.* Berkeley, CA: Ten Spreed Press, 1999.

NOAA. *National Estuarine Inventory Data Atlas.* Washington, DC: National Oceanic Atmospheric Administration, 2002.

Oleksy, Walter. *Mapping the Seas.* New York: Franklin Watts, 2002.

O'Mara, Annie. *Oceans.* Mankato, MN: Bridgestone Books, 2000.

Parker, Steve. *Ocean Life.* Edison, NJ: Chartwell Books, 2001.

Pernetta, John. *Guide to the Oceans.* Tonawanda, NY: Firefly Books, 2004.

Peterson, David, and Christine Peterson. *The Atlantic Ocean.* New York: Children's Press, 2001.

Pinet, Paul. *Invitation to Oceanography.* Sudbury, MA: Jones and Bailtell, 2000.

Prager, Ellen. *The Oceans.* New York: Mcgraw-Hill, 2000.

Sayre, April. *Ocean.* New York: Twenty-First Century Books, 1996.

Scholastic Staff. *Scholastic Atlas of the Oceans.* New York: Scholastic, 2001.

Seon, Manley. *The Oceans: A Treasury of the Sea World.* Garden City, NY: Doubleday, 1997.

Simon, Seymour. *How to Be an Ocean Scientist in Your Own Home.* Emmeryville, CA: J.B. Lippincott, 1998.

Smith, Walter. *The Sea in Motion.* New York: T. Y. Crowell, 1998.

Sonntag, Linda. *Atlas of the Oceans.* Brookfield, CT: Copper Beach Books, 2001.

Stevenson, Robert, and Frank Talbot. *Oceans: The Illustrated Library of the Earth.* Emmaus, PA: Rodale Press, 1996.

Stow, Keith. *Exploring Ocean Sciences.* New York: John Wiley, 1998.

Svarney, Thomas, and Pat Svarney. *The Handy Ocean Answer Book.* New York: Gale Research, 2000.

Thruman, Harold. *Essentials of Oceanography.* Upper Saddle River, NJ: Prentice Hall, 1999.

Index

About the Author

KENDALL HAVEN is an award-winning master storyteller and the author of many books for Libraries Unlimited and Teacher Ideas Press. He has performed for over 3 million children and 900,000 adults in 44 states, and has won numerous awards both for his story-writing and for his story-telling. He has conducted workshops for over 25,000 teachers and 90,000 students from over 800 schools in over 20 states on his revolutionary Write Right! approach to teaching creative and expository writing. Haven is a 7-time winner of the Storytelling World Silver Award for best Story Anthology. He has twice been designated an American Library Association "Notable Recording Artist," and is the only story teller in America with 3 entries in the American Library Association's *Best of the Best for Children*.